A Life of Joy and Accomplishments

From Mother to Administrator,
A Nurse's Journey

Dorothy Meletta George

PINA PUBLISHING 🍍 SEATTLE

PINA PUBLISHING 🍍 SEATTLE

A Life of Joy and Accomplishments
Copyright © 2022 by Dorothy Meletta George
Cover and book design by Susan Harring © 2022 for J.A. Zehrer Group LLC

All rights reserved. No part of this book may be reproduced or transmitted in any form or by any means without written permission from the author.

ISBN: 978-1-943493-56-2 (pbk)
ISBN: 978-1-943493-59-3 (hc)
ISBN: 978-1-943493-58-6 (eBook)

Price Softcover: $9.99
Price Hardcover: $14.99
Price eBook: 2.99
Kindle Unlimited: FREE

Summary:
Like many others, living a life of substance and quality was a dream of Dorothy's. She grew up in Sheboygan, Wisconsin as the youngest of eight children. Being surrounded by a large, loving family inspired her to have a beautiful family of her own. When she met and married her high school sweetheart, Ronnie Manser, she could see her dreams coming true. Thirteen years later, Ronnie and Dorothy both had good jobs, a new home, and five children ages 2-12. Dorothy described their life together as, "busy and wonderful!"

Dorothy worked part-time as a nurse at a local hospital. Ronnie always said, "It isn't for the money, but you never know when you will need your nursing skills." In January of 1970, the unimaginable happened when Ronnie passed away unexpectedly. Dorothy's resiliency shined during this difficult time with the support of her family, her ferocious determination, and her talents in the nursing field.

This book is an autobiography by Dorothy Meletta George. In her own words, she takes you through her personal joys, tragedies, challenges, and triumphs. Dorothy describes her day with Rosa Parks, her unforgettable trip to Greece, and she includes some of her best family recipes.

The biggest lesson she shares in these pages, is the depiction of her transition from darkness to light in her personal and professional life. Dorothy illustrates how she became a Hospital Administrator in a male dominated field, established herself as a nationally known Hospital Accreditation Consultant, and opened her heart to love again.

This book implores you to ask yourself: *am I living my dream?*

[1. Biography & Autobiography/Medical 2. Inspiration & Personal Growth 3. Parenting/Motherhood 4. Hospital Administration & Care 5. Nursing Management & Leadership 6. Self Help Motivational & Inspirational 7. Personal Growth/Happiness]

Dedication

To my family who has helped me through difficult times. I am so proud of all my children and everything they have accomplished in their lives.

Statements from Dorothy's Children

Richard
My mother was ahead of her time in many aspects of her life. Her success in the field of nursing while raising five children is a testament to her drive, passion, and Schnettler stubbornness. This is an inspiring read that shows how one can get through difficult challenges and thrive and still have time to make Sauerbraten.

Lori
What a great, inspirational story. Her life's struggles and successes and how she dealt with them are a great lesson for all. Thank you for the effort you put into your life's story and for all you have done for your family!

Lynn
Great job, mom! You have put a lot of time and dedication into this project and it shows. Should be an interesting read for all.

Juli
Mother, role model, hero, and friend. What a gift to have this collection of stories that remind us of the accomplishments, challenges and fun that encompassed her life. Love you Mom!

David
What we missed out on with our father's early exit, we gained with a lifetime of our mother's love, guidance, her voice, and now her amazing story.

Table of Contents

Chapter 1 - Grandpa Schnettler 11
Chapter 2 - Grandma Schnettler 15
Chapter 3 - Childhood 19
Chapter 4 - High School and College 23
Chapter 5 - Ronald Manser 27
Chapter 6 - Family Growth 29
Chapter 7 - Life with Children 31
Chapter 8 - Ronnie's Death 35
Chapter 9 - Adjusting to Their Dad's Death 39
Chapter 10 - Trips to Madison 43
Chapter 11 - Cub Scouts and Big Brothers 45
Chapter 12 - Green Bay Packers 47
Chapter 13 - St. Nicholas Hospital Experiences 49
Chapter 14 - Stories and Fond Dishes from
              2120 North 26th Street 55
Chapter 15 - Plum Lake 63
Chapter 16 - Harold Enters the Family 65
Chapter 17 - Management Opportunities at
              St. Nicholas Hospital 69
Chapter 18 - Nurse Supervisor Experiences 73
Chapter 19 - Our Move to Arkansas 87
Chapter 20 - QUALvue 93
Chapter 21 - Things I've Made 99
Chapter 22 - Different Paths for the Family 103
Chapter 23 - Packer Fans 107
Chapter 24 - Memorable Trips I've Taken 109
Chapter 25 - Health Issues 113
Chapter 26 - Social Activities in Hot Springs Village 115
Chapter 27 - Moving Back to Wisconsin 117
Chapter 28 - Final Chapter 119

Preface

This is a story of many facts recorded with fiction. There are always possibilities that a story may identify someone famous in life. The intrigue of storytelling supports this possibility and provides the framework for a good story.

Introduction

The quality of life is a mystery that many people have tried to solve over the years. We know that life begins at conception, but when is the true essence of life formed? What defines life? Is it responsibility or is it the quality of the individual activity? Many of us ponder this complex issue.

I am who I am. Each one of us is an individual. Through the years, life has taken me along many paths, some were of my choosing and some were definitely not. We become the individuals we are because of our many experiences. Would I make some different choices if I had known the path down which I would travel? Probably. But that is what makes our lives unique. We don't always have the foresight to know what hand we will be dealt.

My name is Dorothy George and I was born in Sheboygan, Wisconsin on April 3, 1935. My middle name is Meletta. I was actually named after my godmother, whose name was Melitta. When they entered the information on my birth certificate, they made a spelling error and so I went through life with a very unusual middle name simply because of that error in spelling.

Chapter 1

Grandpa Schnettler

My father, Nicholas Schnettler grew up on the family farm. His parents had the first car in the area. He drove the car to dances and at the end of the night he would drive a girl home. Then he'd go back to the dance and drive another girl home. He did this with my mother also. My father called my mother to ask her on a date but she would never go to the phone. She'd always say, "What does he want? What does he want?" Clearly, he eventually won her over.

My father was the superintendent at the Polarware Company in Sheboygan, a locally owned company known for manufacturing high quality commercial cookware. One day he came home with a box of pots and pans that they had made experimentally. The pots were made of three layers. The inner and outer were stainless steel and the middle was copper. Grandma was supposed to try them out to see how they worked. When she fried food in them, it didn't stick like it did in other pans. The company tried making more of them, but they were too expensive to produce. Even though Polarware gave up the project, my mother was allowed to keep the pots and pans and she used them for years. A couple of them are them are still being used by my daughter Lori and son, Richard.

My father loved construction work and building houses of any kind. I was born in the corner house on Cleveland Avenue and 23rd Street (2224 Cleveland Ave.) When I was five, we moved next door into a house which my father also built (2220 Cleveland Ave.) At the time of our move I had the mumps, which were quite common at the time. I was not supposed to leave the house. My older brothers put me in a chair, covered me with a blanket and carried me over to the new house. Years later my father built the white stucco house across the street (2219 Cleveland Ave.) After that he built one on the opposite corner (2204 Cleveland Ave.), which was the house we were living in when I got married. Following that, he built one more on a lot in the middle of the block (2216 Cleveland Ave.) As my brothers and sisters got married, he helped each one of them build a house.

Building houses was quite a family project. In total we built five houses on Cleveland Avenue. The final one (2216 Cleveland Ave.) was the retirement home my parents lived in until my father passed away in 1972. My mother continued living there until about 1985.

2224 Cleveland Ave.

2220 Cleveland Ave.

2219 Cleveland Ave.

2204 Cleveland Ave.

2216 Cleveland Ave.

Chapter 2

Grandma Schnettler

My mother, Helen Burkhart Schnettler, grew up in St. Nazianz. Their homestead was an old house at the bottom of a hill. My parents met while they were in school at St. Gregory's. My father used to drive to my mother's house and coast down the hill to her house with the engine of his car turned off. My mother snuck out of the house, jumped in his car, and away they'd go. After years of dating, they got married and started a family. My mother had her hands full raising seven children. When my father was building houses on Cleveland Avenue, they lived in the garage of one of the houses as it was being built. My mother used to laugh and say she remembered making a lot of meals where there was plaster dust mixed in with all the other ingredients.

William was the fourth son in the family. When he was four months old, my mother's sister, Anna, was babysitting while my mother and father went out for the evening. When they came home, they went to check on the baby. Unfortunately, they found him unresponsive in his crib. My parents called a doctor, who came right away. William had died in his sleep and the doctor told my parents there was nothing that could have been done. This was well before SIDS was given a name.

My mother never got over the death of my brother, William. Decades later, my mother was elderly, widowed, and living with us. My husband, at that time in my life, was Harold. He and I had gone out for one evening and when we came home I heard a noise coming from my mother's bedroom. I went to her room and found her crying. When I asked her what happened, she told me she was still extremely upset over William's death. All those years later she still felt guilty for having gone away that evening. No matter how hard I tried, I could not console her regarding his death.

When my father died unexpectedly of a heart attack, my parents were still living on Cleveland Avenue. My father was in his early 70's at the time. A few years later, my mother started receiving threatening phone calls. A man would call her in the evening and say, "Hello, Helen. How are you? I'm watching you." She decided to go to California to get away from the caller. She spent three months there with my sister Catherine. She thought that would be sufficient time to distance herself from the caller. The night she returned home to Sheboygan, she received a call from the threatening caller. "I see you're home, Helen." My husband Harold and I offered to let her move in with us and she agreed. The last home my father built was sold, and she spent the next several years living with us.

After my mother had lived with us for a few years, I came home from work one night and Harold asked me if I knew my mother was moving out to live with Marion, my sister. Of course, I didn't, so I went and confronted her and she admitted she had gotten an apartment with Marion. She said we were never home and she was lonely. They had already put a down payment on the apartment and bought new furniture.

My mother moved out and lived with my sister for about two weeks when my sister came to see me at work. While sitting in my office, she told me that our mother wanted to move back home with us. She said she was more lonely living with my sister Marion than she was when she lived with us. We moved my mother back in with us. I believe this was around 1988.

After another year or two, my mother decided she wanted to move into a retirement home. I took her to several places and she picked out one she thought she would like to live in. I made the necessary arrangements. Within a month or two they had an opening and she moved in. After being there for several weeks she decided she wanted to move back in with us. This time I said no. She was in the best place for her at the time. She was in her early 90's and would eventually need to be in assisted living.

My mother's birthday was on New Year's Eve. Since she was born on 12/31/1899 it was easy to keep track of her age. In 1980, when she turned 80 years old, a large group of family members gathered to help her celebrate. It was quite the celebration! Every year after that, we had a birthday party for her on the Saturday between Christmas and New Year's Eve. The celebrations got so large that we had over 100 people attending. With those numbers we had no choice but to rent a hall for the annual festivities. The first year my daughter Lynn and her husband John owned Lake Street Cafe in Elkhart Lake, we had a celebration of my mother's birthday and family New

Year's Eve party at their restaurant. Everyone who attended was assigned a job to help with dinner. Some people cooked, some served, and some were on clean-up. Lynn supervised. The young kids were not allowed in the formal dining room. They played and ate in the bar area. The teenage kids babysat them while the adults enjoyed a sit-down dinner in the main dining room. The restaurant was not open to the public, so we had the place to ourselves. That was the night I danced on the bar. Those parties were a lot of fun because it was only family.

Mother died at the age of 98 in 1998.

Chapter 3

Childhood

I had seven brothers and sisters. My mother first had four boys and then four girls. I was the youngest sibling of the family. We grew up on the outskirts of Sheboygan, Wisconsin and raised chickens right in our own yard in a big chicken coop. The only pet I ever had was a black chicken named Blackie. When he got quite large, my parents thought it would be better if he went out to the farm. He will have more freedom to run, my mother explained. I know why he went out to the farm… he was someone's dinner!

We were a large family living in a very small house on the edge of town. We spent most of our time playing outside with the neighbor kids. My sister Gert and I had a group of friends that we played with. We didn't have a lot of toys. In fact, I didn't have a bike until I was in my early teens. My first bike turned out to be my sister Marion's hand-me down bike.

I went to kindergarten at Jefferson School at the age of four. It was several miles from my home. We walked to school and back every day, rain or shine. There was never any fear of what might happen to us.

I started first grade at St. Dominic's Catholic School, which was about a half block from my home. It certainly was convenient. I spent eight years there. The nuns at St. Dominic's were an important part of our lives. They enjoyed spending time with families in the area. At our house there was a big open area that had been a racetrack at one time. In the winter it was so flat that when the snow melted and refroze, we had a perfectly formed skating pond that we used to race one another. We built bonfires and all the neighbors spent afternoons and evenings skating and keeping warm by the bonfire. One of the nuns borrowed a pair of our skates and joined in the fun. It was quite a site seeing a nun, in full religious habit, ice skating in winter and playing baseball in summer.

When I finished fifth grade, my brother Bob returned from spending several years in the Navy. Several months later my father and brothers began building a house across the street from where we lived. The ditch for the sewer was dug by hand by my brothers. One day, while digging, the side of the ditch collapsed. Bob was buried alive. Several fire engines and police cars were sent to the site. The nuns pulled me from class and sent me home because they were fearful of how this could end. Fortunately, Bob saw the cave-in coming. He trapped air under his arms so he could breathe until they dug him out. He was in the hospital overnight. His only complaint was that none of the nurses were very pretty.

I wasn't always the best little girl. I remember drying corn silk, wrapping it in newspaper and smoking it like a cigarette behind the neighbor's garage. My grandfather made wine and I remember sitting behind the furnace, drinking his wine with my older brothers and sisters.

We used to play a lot of baseball. On Sunday mornings after church, all the neighbor kids and their fathers gathered in an empty lot to play baseball. The mothers were all home cooking dinner. We always had fried chicken for dinner at noon on Sundays.

In summer we went to St. Nazianz, Wisconsin which is about 30 miles northwest of Sheboygan. Most of my relatives lived there. The kids played outside while the parents visited or played cards inside. We spent a lot of time playing in the haylofts in the barns. The old family homestead in St. Nazianz was a small house that had several additions added over the years. The bedrooms upstairs were very small; one for the boys and one for the girls. I remember my cousin slept in a crib until he was quite old. He hung his legs over the rails because he was too big. Unfortunately for him, there was no room in the bedroom for another bed.

In the summertime I spent several weeks there also, at my cousin's home. On especially hot days we walked to Pigeon Lake, which was several miles away. We walked back as well. Our cousins also came to Sheboygan to spend time with us during the summer.

While in high school we lived about 2 miles away from school. We walked to school, home for lunch, back again, and then home after school was over. Walking was considered safe. We never had any trouble, unlike today's times.

Chapter 4

High School and College

As a senior in high school, I remember being called into the counselor's office after taking an aptitude test. I earned one of the highest test scores for secretarial capabilities. One of the last things I wanted to do was work as a secretary. The year was 1953 and there were not many choices for women. The accepted choices were secretarial, teaching, or nursing. I opted for nursing, much to the chagrin of my counselor. At the time I looked at it as the lesser of three evils. Having already rejected the idea of secretarial work, I also felt I was not cut out to be a teacher. The only option left was nursing.

Elkhart Lake, Wisconsin is a beautiful little resort town where many people go to vacation. There are several lakes in the area. Another main attraction is Road America, a nationally known racetrack that attracts many wealthy families from the Milwaukee and Chicago areas. During the summers of 1952-54, I worked as a waitress at a restaurant in Elkhart Lake, earning money for my education. My base pay was minimal, but the tips were good. During those summers, I earned enough to pay for my nursing education which cost a total of $350. At that time this was a considerable amount of money. Also, some of our nursing education was subsidized by the work that we did in the hospital.

We had a lot of fun working in Elkhart Lake. We each had one waitress uniform. When we were done working in the evening, we grabbed a bar of soap and a change of clothes. We went down and jumped in the lake with our uniforms on. We dove in a few times and our uniforms were clean. We hung them up to dry on the deck or in the cottage. Then we went out and partied for a few hours. We usually had one day off during the week. We also did a lot of babysitting. We really had quite active summers.

I entered St. Mary's Catholic School of Nursing in Milwaukee, Wisconsin in August of 1953. It is funny how certain events are clear in one's memory so many years later. The first evening some of my new friends were discussing how they worked as nurse's aides prior to entering nursing school. They talked and laughed about someone they had worked with who had put a bedpan under a patient backwards. I quietly sat by listening, since I had never seen a bedpan and wouldn't know which was the front or back!

There were 56 students in our class. Our dormitory rooms had single beds, and a closet with a sink in it. Bathrooms with toilets and showers were down at the end of the hall. My roommate was Laurie Schuster. I also became very close friends with Jo Lobotski (Hanson), Judy Martin (McClutchy) and Pauline (Polly) Joerres (McCormick). We spent a lot of time together, going to movies or going for long walks. These girls became lifelong friends.

One of the first questions in our first class was asked by our instructor, Ms. Newman. "How do you clean a bar of soap?" she asked. We quickly learned that you just hold it under water and wash the outer layer off. This was my introduction into nursing, a field that I knew absolutely nothing about. And to think, I had chosen it only because it sounded better than teaching or secretarial work.

The standards at the school were very high and we felt like we were being treated like prisoners. Our uniforms were severely starched. So much so, that after the starching and pressing we had to "crack" them open to loosen them up. To "crack a uniform" meant that the front was pulled apart to loosen the tight, starched bodice. We were required to wear hairnets and absolutely no makeup. My years of nursing school were tedious and demanding, but I made some lifelong friends through it all.

Prior to entering nursing school, I had always found Catholic nuns to be loving, caring people. I quickly changed my opinion. The Director of the School of Nursing was a tyrant and a nun who was hard to love. Because of her, I never really bonded with the school. Even so, to this day I am thankful for receiving a first-rate nursing education.

Having been raised in a very strict family, I tried to be obedient and was afraid to do anything out of line. I never got in trouble and finished one of the top five students in my class. At the time, I felt the director punished the good students and was compassionate and understanding to those who got in trouble or struggled in their classes. Looking back, I believe this gave her the opportunity to show them her love and empathy during difficult situations. As far as the rest of us were concerned, I believe that this was her way to make us humble and obedient.

I remember one Christmas Eve around 4 p.m., when I was called into her office. The director asked me to be seated and informed me that I would not be able to go home for Christmas. I was needed to stay in the dorm, to be family to those who had to work over the holiday. I had worked nights the entire week before, as well as attending class during the day to make it possible for me to go home for the holidays. My fiancé was picking me up at 5:00 p.m. After leaving the director's office in tears, I went to my room, laid on my bed, and cried. She called me back to her office half an hour later and informed me that if I was so selfish and was only going to think about myself, I could go home if I wanted. The director said I should think long and hard about what I was doing. I decided to go home, but I never forgot the cruelty of this act. Out of more than 50 members in my class, no one else had been asked to stay at school when they had the holiday off.

One of our requirements for nursing school was to go on "affiliations". Affiliations were trainings at different hospitals, in different areas. Most of the time that we went on affiliations, my friends from college and I went at the same time. Those nursing school clinicals took me to: the Children's Hospital in Milwaukee, a psychiatric hospital in St. Louis, Missouri, and to Muirdale Tuberculosis Sanitarium in Milwaukee. We spent about three months training at each. When we graduated in August 1956, we had all our classroom education along with many hours of hands-on experience in hospitals.

Chapter 5

Ronald Manser

In high school I was part of a group of guys and gals that hung out together. After a while some of us started pairing off. I married my high school sweetheart, Ronald Manser, on October 13, 1956.

Ronnie grew up in Sheboygan, Wisconsin. His parents, Joe and Bunnie, had two children. Ron was the oldest and he had a younger sister named Sue. They lived in an apartment above Bunnie's sister on Trimberger Court in Sheboygan. They lived there while Ronnie was growing up and then they moved into a house that was owned by Ronnie's aunt. Ronnie never had a car until he graduated from high school and entered the service.

Before that we walked or took the bus whenever we needed or wanted to go out. He left the car for his father to use while he was in the service. We reclaimed it when we moved back to Sheboygan years later.

Ronnie joined the Army after graduating from high school. When we got married, we left immediately for Fort Carson, Colorado, where he was stationed. We were there until February 1957, when he was discharged. At that time, we left Colorado and moved back to Sheboygan. I went to work at St. Nicholas Hospital and Ronnie started working at Garton Toy Company in Sheboygan. We moved into an apartment on Calumet Drive. He was not happy with working in a factory and started looking for other job opportunities. He studied to become an insurance agent and was quickly hired by Schils Insurance Agency. The company later merged with Ballschmider and it became Ballschmider-Schils. Ronnie became their office manager.

Chapter 6

Family Growth

Richard, our oldest son, was born July 15, 1957, in Sheboygan at St. Nicholas Hospital. Lori followed two years later on June 26, 1959. Lynn was born September 5, 1960.

Richard, Lori, and Lynn were all born when we were living in that first apartment on Calumet Drive. It was very small and cramped. Emma was the owner and she lived below us on the first floor. Emma loved having Richard follow her around, especially when she was working in the garden. However, there was one time when Richard picked all the green tomatoes and proudly brought them to me and called them apples. "Emma's aahpples" as he called them.

We moved into our new house on 26th Street in 1962.

Juli was born on May 27, 1964. David, our youngest, was born July 20, 1966.

On Ronnie's side of the family, his only sibling, Sue had 13 children: 11 boys and 2 girls. The oldest is a year younger than Juli.

Chapter 7

Life with Children

I continued working part time at St. Nicholas Hospital. Every time the sixth week of maternity leave was up, the phone rang. The nuns called asking when I would be coming back to work. I usually went back after the six weeks.

At that time our family was considered small. Most of my

brothers and sisters had families larger than ours. Marion was my only sibling that had fewer children, she had four. And Ronnie's sister, Sue, had the largest with 13.

In summers, at least once a week, all my sisters got together with all our kids to have a picnic and baseball game. Since we had so many children there were always enough players for two full teams. Occasionally other cousins that didn't live in our area came and joined us.

Life with five children was busy and wonderful. I always worked evenings or nights so Ronnie was with the kids. The children loved when I worked because then they had party night with dad. I usually worked from 6:00 p.m. to 11:00 p.m.

In 1962, a subdivision was being built in the North 26th Street area of Sheboygan. They were selling lots and Ronnie and I bought one. We had our house built by a prefab home builder. To help cut down on expenses, Grandpa Schnettler, my father, built all the cabinets and worked on the electrical while Grandpa Manser, Ronnie's father, did most of the painting. Richard, Lori, and Lynn played in the sand and ran around the nearby wooded area while I worked on the house, varnishing cabinets and painting walls. We moved into the house in October 1962.

My sister Gert's family lived on 25th Street, one block away from our house. When Gert was going into the hospital to have her sixth child, I stayed at their house and served dinner to their kids and mine, which was a total of 10 kids. Her husband Bill was anxiously waiting at the hospital to find out if they were going to have a son because their other five children were girls.

As it started getting dark, Bill drove into the driveway, got out of his car with a big smile on his face and I yelled, "It's a boy!" He was grinning from ear to ear.

Chapter 8

Ronnie's Death

Tragedy hit on Tuesday, January 27, 1970, when Ronnie, the love of my life, died unexpectedly. That night, my dad, Grandpa Schnettler, called and said he was going to pick the kids up to watch a show on TV. At that time, we only had a black and white television and he had a new colored TV set. He picked up the kids after supper and Ronnie and I were home alone. We stayed home because Ronnie was not feeling well due to a bad cold. I was in the living room working on papers for work when I heard a strange sound from the bedroom upstairs. When I went to see what it was, I found Ronnie taking his last breath. I called one of the neighbors because we didn't have 911 at the time. They called the doctor from an emergency unit, but by the time they arrived it was too late. They were unable to revive him.

When I was at the hospital, they asked whether I wanted an autopsy done. I was in such shock that I thought if they didn't do an autopsy, he would be okay the next day. So, we never found out what caused his death. This is one of my biggest regrets. If the cause of death was determined, this would have been great health information for my children and grandchildren. Ronnie was only 34 years old at the time of his death.

I was in shock over my high school sweetheart and now husband's death. At the age of 34, I was a widow with five children, ages three to twelve, to raise on my own. Strangely, it was almost as if he had a premonition that something was going to happen. The Sunday evening before, Ronnie and I talked about what we would do if something happened to the other one. He talked about which funeral home I was to call, etc. At the time of his death, I immediately followed through with Ronnie's requested arrangements.

Although I had dealt with death in the nursing profession, I had no idea what it really entailed. The day of the funeral, I remember everyone saying their good-byes and walking out the door. I was alone. I stood with my back to the door, wondering how I was going to manage, and what I was going to do with the rest of my life. I had never before and have never since, felt so alone. The responsibility of raising five children seemed overwhelming and impossible.

I immediately went through the anger stage in the grieving process. I railed against my husband for leaving me with five children to raise by myself. We had talked about having a big family, but I never dreamt I would be doing it by myself.

At the funeral, Richard was told by many people that he now had to be the "man of the family". This was a terrible burden to place on a 12 year-old. He tried very hard for the first year or two. Then apparently, he entered his anger stage of the grieving process. He didn't speak to me for a year or so, all the while living under the same roof. We had some very difficult years. My mother kept saying, "One of you is not going to make it, one of you has to give in." Gradually our relationship improved over time.

Chapter 9

Adjusting to Their Dad's Death

We quickly had to adjust to life "without dad". I remember telling the children many times how fortunate they were to have had such a good dad, even though his years with them were limited. I couldn't cry because it upset the children, so I learned to keep my feelings to myself. I can still picture Richard, my oldest son, standing before me saying, "I will do anything you want mom, just don't cry." I believe they needed to rely on my strength to cope and survive. Seeing me cry weakened this resolve. I know now that this is not healthy. However, sometimes we deal with difficulty the best way we know how. I don't believe there were grief counselors in 1970. If there were, I certainly wasn't aware of them. I tried to comfort my children, but I was also working through the grief process myself and did not always do the right thing.

Prior to Ronnie's death, he had always encouraged me to work part-time. He always said, "It isn't for the money, but you never know when you will need your nursing skills." Little did I know how right he would be. I was working two nights a week at St. Nicholas Hospital when he died. Without

Ronnie there and because of the age of the children, my niece Vicki, who was in high school at the time, stayed at the house on the night that I worked. This worked quite well until the children got older and felt they didn't need a babysitter. I felt they needed an adult presence in the house to supervise their comings and goings during the evenings so, at that point, I changed to the day shift.

Each one of the children experienced the loss of their father at different stages in their life. Richard was in his teens when he became very angry. Lori, at the age of 10, cried the most at the funeral. She seemed to let go the best of all the children. Lynn, age 9 dealt with her dad's death in her own way. I was told not to bring Juli, age 5 and David, age 3 to the funeral home or funeral because they were too young. To this day I am sorry I took that advice. Juli and David had the most difficulty facing the reality of their father's death. If I could advise anyone how to handle this situation, I would tell them to face life head on. Let the children experience life no matter what age they are, or the circumstances of the death. Children are very resilient. In hindsight, I wish I could go back and take them to the funeral home to say their good-byes to their father.

While in middle school, the father of a dear friend of David's died after a long battle with diabetes and heart problems. During the visitation at the funeral home, David collapsed and had to be helped by Harold and myself. He was totally distraught seeing his friend's father in a casket. This memory stays with me, even to this day.

Another incident involving David was when he was a teenager. We were moving into a different house and I had asked him to clean up some things in the attic. When I came home from work, I heard wrenching sobs coming from the attic. I found David sitting up there with his father's personal belongings that I had kept. He was mourning the death of his father, 14 years after Ronnie had died.

We were always looking for things to do to keep busy, especially on weekends. One weekend we decided to go camping with our good friends, George and Lollie, and their kids Greg and Brooke. George and Lollie pulled their camper to a campground near Plymouth, WI called Rocky Knoll. The children and I followed in our station wagon. As we were getting the camper set up and the food arranged, a big storm came up. We hadn't put up the tent yet and the storm hit so fast that we didn't have time to put things away properly. We quickly put some things in the back of the station wagon. George and Richard jumped into the station wagon and the rest of us got into the camper. The storm continued for several hours. Finally, we decided we were just going to have to go to sleep where we were. When we got up in the morning, we gathered the food we could find in the camper and made breakfast. Richard and George did the same in the station wagon. Later, we heard George complaining about the lousy cereal that we had brought along. He told me the cereal I bought for the kids was terrible. As the day went on, we realized that the lousy cereal turned out to be our dog Heidi's food. To this day George still gets teased about eating dog food.

We took trips to Milwaukee to spend weekends with my friends from college. They had children the same ages as mine. All the children played together while the adults visited. We also took trips to Chicago to visit my brother Nick and his family. They had an indoor pool that the kids loved to play in.

Chapter 10

Trips to Madison

When Juli was seven years old, she became extremely thin even though it seemed she was eating everything in sight. When everyone else finished eating she ate the rest of the food off the platters. One day she was with Gene Smith, a good friend of ours. He noticed she was having difficulty outside with the brightness. I took her to the doctor, and she was diagnosed with hyperthyroidism. This was extremely unusual in a child but it can be triggered by an emotional trauma. I took her to the Pediatric Clinic at University Hospital in Madison. It took several years to stabilize her on medication (Propylthiouracyl). Decades later, I am amazed that I still remember the name of her medication.

When Juli was ten, the doctors in Madison decided they wanted to do a thyroidectomy on her. I went home and discussed it with one of the surgeons at St. Nicholas Hospital. Because of her age and the fact that she adjusted well on the medication, he advised that we wait. I'm glad I took his advice because she eventually outgrew the problem.

One of the fun things about this situation was our trips back and forth to Madison. One day we had car trouble. Another car stopped and the gentleman inside offered to help us. After talking for a bit, we learned he was a state senator. As we got into the car, I told Juli, "This is something you should never do. You should never get into a car with a stranger." He helped us contact a garage where they proceeded to tow our car and make the necessary repairs.

Often, on our way back from Madison, we stopped in Fond du Lac for something to eat. The waitresses were always anxious to see Juli come in. They were so impressed that such a thin little girl could eat so much.

Chapter 11

Cub Scouts and Big Brothers

It was interesting how different people treated us after Ronnie's death. One interesting situation was with David, as a Cub Scout. At one of the meetings, I was informed that each month one of the fathers was expected to take all of the boys on a field trip. I was told in no uncertain terms that just because David didn't have a father, it didn't leave me off the hook. I was expected to take my turn. I talked to my brother Bob about it because I was a little upset. He said he would take care of everything. Bob had a trout pond on his property. He told me to bring the boys out on the day of the field trip. He let them all fish and catch trout. He also had his four sons there to help. Each boy was allowed to catch two fish, which my nephews cleaned and packaged for them to take home. One little boy didn't have any idea what fishing was about and tried to spear the fish with the end of the pole. We taught him how to fish and helped him catch his two fish that he was allowed. When my nephews had them packaged and ready to take home, the small boy asked, "Do you get two fish also? Can I catch two for you?" He was so excited to catch his first fish.

David was also involved with the Big Brother Organization. His Big Brother's name was Dale. He came to our house to be introduced to our family. We had a nice long conversation learning each other's likes and dislikes. David was just a little boy, about 6 years old and Dale was a grown man, over 6 feet tall. When it was time for Dale to leave, David jumped up, ran to the closet, and got Dale's coat. David held the coat by the arms trying to give Dale a chance to put the coat on. We all ended up laughing because there was no way this little boy was going to be able to hold the coat for this grown man.

Chapter 12

Green Bay Packers

When Ronnie and I got married he was an avid football fan and golfer. At that time, I had a choice of doing both with him or he said he would find buddies to do them with. Needless to say, I became a golfer and a football fan.

In 1969, the Green Bay Packers extended the seating at Lambeau Field and we put in a request to purchase season tickets. In December 1969 we received notice that we were getting four tickets. Ronnie died in January 1970 and he never got a chance to use the tickets.

Being as angry as I was at the time, I almost gave up the tickets. I'm very thankful that I never did because we enjoyed many games as a family. The children, still to this day, enjoy going to see the Green Bay Packers play at Lambeau Field.

Chapter 13

St. Nicholas Hospital Experiences

When I graduated in 1956, my first job was in my hometown at St. Nicholas Hospital. This was probably the rudest awakening of my career. The restrictions and controls that were in place at a teaching hospital were much stricter than in a community hospital. We had an intravenous nurse who started all the IV's because at that time they were very sparse. A medicine nurse gave any intramuscular medications. She had a list with patient's room numbers and just went down the list and gave out the drugs. If someone went home and another patient was admitted to the room, I always wondered if they got the medication on the list from the previous patient.

This was a short period of employment due to Ronnie and I getting married several months later and moving to Colorado. When he was discharged the following year we returned to Sheboygan. We had just had our first child when I was rehired to work at St. Nicholas Hospital. I started working the evening shift which started at 6:00 p.m. The other nurses had left at 3:00 or 4:00 p.m. The only nurse in attendance was a nun, plus nursing assistants. When we came on at 6:00 p.m. there was no one to give us a report. The documentation on the charts was minimal. Often, there wasn't even an admission diagnosis, so we went to the patients and asked them what they were in the hospital for. Patient information was available on the Kardex, which was a recording system on paper. We just hoped that it was up to date.

We filled our own oral pills from bottles in the nursing station. I remember getting patients ready for bed, always having a small box in my pocket with sleeping pills (Tuinal, Seconal, Nembutal, etc.). We also carried a few Empirin #3's, as these were the oral pain medication of choice at that time. If a patient asked for a sleeping pill and none was on their Kardex we asked what color they had the night before and gave them one accordingly. I do not remember any restrictions on sedatives and if there were, they were very loose.

Nursing to me was always a challenge. I never got used to the death and dying process. Due to personal experience, I knew what families went through when a loved one died. One specific situation that I remember was the admission of a man who was dying of cancer. He watched the Packer game during the day and was fully alert, but throughout the night he regressed steadily. The next day he was in the final stages of dying. The admitting nurse was a young woman who had never seen a patient die. As her boss, I felt I needed to help her through the process so that she would be the best support possible for the family. The family members were so frightened, they sat back and were afraid to touch the man or be anywhere near him. Through the course of the day, I encouraged them to hold him, touch him, hug him, and do whatever they wanted to, since this was their last chance to have personal contact with him. By the time he died, he had been in the arms of the entire family. This experience led to the development of "Family Rooms" within the hospital.

The number of patients at the hospital was declining because people were no longer staying for extended periods of time and empty beds were available. At that time, there was no end-of-life care like "hospice" as we know it today. I proposed to the Hospital Administrator that we take two rooms, put a doorway between them, and furnish one as a "Family Room". I suggested we furnish it with a couch, microwave, and immediate needs for families who were staying around the clock. My administrator agreed and we created the "Family Room" at no extra charge to the families.

The hospital received generous donations from many families. Memorial funds were given for the expansion of the service of "Family Rooms". Eventually one was put in each medical/surgical department. After a seriously ill young child's family spent many days in the "Family Room", they eventually funded a "Family Room" in the Pediatric Unit. The hospital, to my knowledge, provides this service to families to this day. We were so proud to initiate this practice so many years ago.

When I was a manager in the hospital, I had nuns and laity working for me. One week I had a disagreement with one of the nuns. She had committed numerous errors while on duty and I felt I needed to speak to her superior. I told her boss that I felt she was a danger to the patients and asked her what she wanted me to do. She said if the nun was a danger to the patients, I needed to fire her and encouraged me to do so. During the following week I proceeded to terminate her. Needless to say,

A Life of Joy and Accomplishments

she was very upset with me. The next Saturday evening, Harold, my husband, and I went to the 5:00 p.m. mass. Shortly after we entered our pew, three nuns came in and sat directly in front of us. One of them was the nun I had just terminated. At the point of mass when parishioners shake hands and wish each other peace, everyone participated except her. I felt that during mass was not the time to hold grudges. I decided to put an end to this immediately and reached over to tap her on the shoulder. Just as my arm reached her shoulder, she turned toward me. My finger caught in the veil of her habit and I accidentally jerked it off her head. It landed in the pew behind her. She started to laugh and said, "That's OK George" and turned back to pray. Harold and I started laughing and couldn't stop. We had been assigned to distribute communion and as we walked up to the alter, we both had trouble containing our giggles.

Another of my experiences was being given the responsibility for the Social Service Department. When St. Nicholas built their new hospital in Sheboygan, Wisconsin, two rooms were allocated in the basement for women who were admitted through the Emergency Room for domestic abuse. To me, it was like being put in a dungeon. These women were already in a fragile state and being put in the "basement apartment" with their children made the situation worse. The children had nothing to do, nothing to play with. They were very restless and screamed and cried. It was very traumatic to see this.

Being given responsibility for this process, since it was under the Social Services Department, I immediately started looking for another way to deal with the situation. I found several individuals and organizations in the community who were interested in opening an independent domestic violence shelter.

The hospital was situated on a city block with several homes surrounding it. The intention of the administration was to buy up the homes as they became vacated or for sale. I petitioned for them to give me one of those vacant homes to use as a shelter and was granted the opportunity. I immediately hired a full-time director who was living in Omaha, Nebraska. Following her hiring, we hired another employee and moved the shelter into a home in proximity of the hospital.

When women came into the Emergency Room for domestic abuse, they were admitted into the house which we named "Safe Harbor". Some of us volunteered to cover shifts so we had 24-hour staffing anytime someone was in residence. We were so successful that we began to outgrow the shelter. We did a feasibility study to determine whether we would be able to buy a home independent of the hospital to house more women. The cost of the study was funded by one of our volunteers. The results determined that we would be able to support an independent facility and therefore one was purchased. As an independent facility, we were governed by a Board of Directors and I was the President of the Board. Unfortunately, I left the Sheboygan area for different employment prior to completion of the project.

Every year the Sheboygan Pine Hills Country Club had a female Pro-Am golf tournament. Martha Nause, who was a golf pro, grew up in Sheboygan, and was the daughter of one of the hospital physicians. Hence, it was called the Martha Nause Golf Tournament. The tournament started around 1989. Proceeds from the tickets sold to play in the tournament went to the Safe Harbor shelter. Because I was the President of the Board, I got to play in the tournament. I didn't win anything;

however, I did sink several long putts which even impressed the golf pro who played with us.

I was employed at St. Nicholas Hospital for over 35 years. I found that any time there was a job to be done and they didn't know who to give it to, they gave it to me. This happened when the fund development person resigned. I was given the responsibility for fund development and I knew absolutely nothing about it. I was sent to a seminar in Washington D.C. with a secretary who was to work with me.

I discovered immediately that the main thing you have to do with fund development is ask people for money. Those who can provide will do so if they are asked. During my first year in this position, the amount of money donated/gifted went up dramatically. When I needed something, I would invite one of the main contributors to the hospital and we would have lunch in my office. After we finished with lunch and small talk, they would ask, "Okay, Dorothy, what do you need?" Next, they would ask if I needed the check right that day or if it could wait until Friday when they wrote foundation checks. When getting thousands of dollars from a donor, I was very willing to wait until Friday.

Chapter 14

Stories and Fond Dishes from 2120 North 26ᵗʰ Street

Our family had an ice cream maker and we liked to make homemade ice cream. (Appendix A) We made it quite often because it always turned out so well and it was fun to do. Once, when we were at Schmidler's Drug Store, we saw a recipe for homemade root beer. We thought it would be fun to make that also. We saved bottles for several weeks, washed them, and ran them through a cycle in the dishwasher. We mixed all the ingredients together and then we bottled it.

We learned one bit of important information. The bottles needed to be tempered to handle the pressure that built up inside. This was very evident when I got a phone call around midnight at work from Harold. We had made our first batch of root beer and one of the bottles exploded. The ceiling in the basement was coated in root beer. From then on we only used beer bottles. We found that any regular glass bottles could not take the pressure that built up from the yeast when it was fermenting. We ordered a bottle capper through Montgomery Ward and filled the beer bottles, leaving some room for air extraction. We took turns capping them and laid them on their sides for 3-4 days as directed in the recipe.

We planned a party for David's eighth grade graduation. David invited all his graduation class and friends. When his friends arrived, David told them that there were coolers outside with drinks in them and they could help themselves. Soon we heard the door swing open and one of his friends ran in yelling, "Your parents are letting us have beer for the party?" From then on we laughed about having friends over for a bottle of root beer/beer out on the deck. (Appendix B)

We grew kohlrabi right out our back door. It was fun to go outside, pull it out of the ground, peel it and eat it like an apple. We also made creamed kohlrabi, which we all enjoyed.

Sauerkraut was another thing we liked to make. The cabbage was packed in large crocks and had to ferment for a long time. The first time we made it, Richard came running up from the basement to tell me that the sauerkraut had spoiled. Being the hard worker that Richard was, he took the crock out and buried it in the back yard. When I found out I was quite upset. Sauerkraut must ferment and the film over the top is the protective layer for the kraut while it is fermenting. Richard had thrown all of it away thinking that it had spoiled. We had to make another batch, which was very tasty.

We used to buy a side of beef since this was more economical. We cut it into portions, wrapped it in packages and stored it in a big freezer in the garage. One time I took the tongue, cut it in chunks, and made beef stroganoff with it. Richard came home from work and was excited because he loved beef stroganoff.

He ate a big plateful. When he was finished eating, we all started laughing. We knew how much he disliked tongue. When we told him what we made the stroganoff out of he was quite upset. He wouldn't eat any more, but he quickly got over the prank that was played on him.

We ate a lot of venison and most of it came from my dad and my brother Bob. They went hunting every year and sometimes they brought Richard along. My father was a good hunter and typically brought home a deer every hunting season. One year they butchered the deer they got at the original Poly Vinyl plant, a company owned by my brother Bob and my brother-in-law Dick. We also got venison from neighbors who knew we really enjoyed it. We made sauerbraten out of it. My father also hunted rabbits and squirrels, which provided other forms of meat for the family. Squirrel and rabbit were prepared basically the same as the venison. Having this influx of meat was very important to our big family because of the amount of food we ate. I still enjoy venison to this day.

Every year several family members went to Midnight Mass on Christmas Eve. After mass we met at my parent's house for venison steak sandwiches.

Ring-a-lings were a pastry that my mother twisted and frosted. We went over after church on Sunday morning to have them.

My mother's Sauerbraten was delicious. No one else knew how to make it but her. One time I wanted to make Sauerbraten for Ronnie but I but didn't have the recipe. I had an idea, I called my parents and invited them for dinner. Venison had to marinade for a week before it was cooked so during the afternoon I got it out, cut it up, and put it in a casserole dish. When my mother arrived for dinner, I asked her what ingredients I needed to make the marinade. By the time we were done, the marinade was complete and I had the recipe! I poured it over the venison, covered it and put it in the refrigerator. I invited them for dinner the following week and cooked the meat for all of us. Some side dishes that my mother always made with Sauerbraten were mashed potatoes, creamed cabbage, and homemade apple sauce. (Appendix C)

A regular stop for me was the Hostess Outlet Store. I bought big boxes of Twinkies and Cupcakes to put in the freezer. When McDonalds had a sale on their burgers we bought a bunch and froze them too.

Our neighbor, Terry Johnson, used to make go-carts and race them in local Soap Box Derby competitions. He had an extra set of wheels laying around so Richard bought them from him. All the neighbor kids decided to make a go-cart, so they used long screws to attach the back axle to a wood frame. The front axle was held on with one screw in the center so the go-cart could be steered. The new wheels were added onto the ends of the axles. The back axle was held on with two screws. One of them was put on upside down so it was sticking up. Richard volunteered to do the test run. He was going around a corner and slid across the screw that was sticking up. The screw tore a hole in his pants and ripped his butt open. He had to go to the emergency room and have stitches. Needless to say, he stood in the back seat of the car on the way home from the hospital.

One day Juli picked tulips for me and brought them home.

When I asked where they came from Juli proudly confessed she got them from our neighbor, Mrs. Adams, garden.

Usually once a week, Ronnie's cousin Billy came to have dinner with us. He rode the bus to the Dairy Queen on Calumet Drive, bought a big bag of Dilly Bars, and then walked over to the house with them. We joked and called them "Billy" Bars.

There were a lot of kids in the neighborhood. My sister Gert and her family lived two blocks away. During the day the kids met up with their friends and were told to be home for dinner. Off they went and we wouldn't see them until later in the day. In the evenings the kids played kick-the-can and ran all around the neighborhood.

George and Lollie Schmidbauer were good friends of ours. They had a dog and our kids loved it. All we ever heard about was how the kids wanted a dog of their own. One year I decided to get them a dog for Christmas. We had dog sat for several friend's dogs and one that we fell in love with was a Schnauzer. We purchased a puppy and it stayed with George and Lollie for several days before Christmas. While we went to church on Christmas Eve, George took the dog's cage and all her belongings to our house and set them up under the tree. When we got home the children were shocked to see a live puppy under the tree. They immediately got the leash out, put it on the dog and took her for a walk. We named her Heidi. Richard took her under his wing and trained her. She was a good friend to the children and they loved her very much. Once the children were at school full time, we could not leave Heidi home all day. Some friends of ours also had a Schnauzer and they asked if they could have Heidi as a companion for their dog. The dogs got along well and became good friends so we moved Heidi to their house. We always missed her at our home but we knew it was better for her to be there, than to be alone all day at our house.

Weekends were always fun because we would get out and go for hikes at Mauthe Lake, Parnell Tower, and Harrington Beach State Park. On Friday nights we would go to Fish Fry's and Brat Fry's.

Richard had a hobby of making model cars. He spent many days and nights in the basement painting and assembling them. He had quite a collection. Richard also had a girlfriend named Ruth. One night they were at Long Lake camping with some high school friends and got busted for being in a tent together. The Park Ranger called Ruth's dad and me to let us know they were banished from the park. Richard got to drive home but Ruth's dad had to go out to the park and pick her up.

Around 1981 we decided to make some changes to our yard. The layout of the land was such that it would be perfect to put in an above-ground swimming pool. We had a construction crew come in and dig out the ground and put in supports for the pool walls. My nephew, Jim Schnettler, oversaw all the work that was being done. Once the plumbing was completed and the pool was constructed we began to build the deck and fencing around it. We made a deal with my nephew, John Rupnick, that if he helped David stain the deck and fencing he could have unlimited use of the pool.

The pool was a great addition and we used it a lot. One of the most memorable times was when Lori and Gary got married.

We had their wedding reception in the back yard. Ronnie's cousin Billy was a florist and he provided floral arrangements that floated in the pool. It was quite stunning.

Chapter 15

Plum Lake

One of the main traditions we had every summer was a trip to Plum Lake in northern Wisconsin. Over the years, most of our extended family participated in vacationing there. Also, some of my college friends and their families joined us at Plum Lake. All the cottages were rented by family members or friends at Froelich's Resort in Sayner, WI for at least two weeks in July. My brothers Nick, Jerry, Bob and their wives Connie, Joan, and Betty, and my sister Catherine and her husband Dick all had speed boats. They brought them up each year so we had several boats available for water skiing. The adults spent the morning playing golf at Plum Lake Golf Course. The afternoons were spent water skiing with all the kids. They would all line up next to the raft, waiting for their turn to water ski. I spent many hours in the water teaching them how to ski. In the evenings we had many cookouts and the kids ran freely throughout the resort to each of the cabins.

There was one small cottage that we nicknamed "The Honeymoon Cottage" where Grandma and Grandpa stayed. Every morning Grandpa walked up to Pat's Bait Shop and cashed in his bills for dimes. Every time one of the grandkids walked by him they got a dime for an ice cream from Grandpa. He also drove into St. Germain and got donuts so that when everyone got up in the morning there were fresh apple fritters on the breakfast table in their cabin. During the hours of the day that weren't occupied with other activities the kids all congregated in the Rec Room which was located next to our cabin. Once the kids were settled in for the night, the adults went to the local pub. Gert, Catherine, and I provided entertainment as "The Ding-A-Ling Sisters". To me, this was one of the most fun traditions that the family had.

Chapter 16

Harold Enters the Family

On afternoon, my friend Vivian and I went to pick up her daughter who worked at a motel in downtown Sheboygan. She wasn't quite finished with her work so we went into the bar to have a drink while we waited for her. Vivian recognized two men and introduced me to them. One of them was Harold George. A couple of nights later Harold called me and asked me out on a date. I said no because I had too much on my plate raising five kids. I had no time to start dating anyone. However, Harold was very persistent. He kept calling and calling, asking me to go out with him. I kept telling the kids to tell him that I wasn't home. Finally, I consented to date him.

I dated Harold for several years. We thought we would never get married because of our differences in religion, plus the fact that he was divorced. He had two young girls from his previous marriage named Terrie and Tammie. At some point I was surprised to find out that Harold went to see a priest at Holy Name Church to discuss our situation. He found out that it was possible for him to get an annulment through the Catholic Church, which would allow us to get married.

After the issue of the annulment was resolved, we got married on November 26, 1976, at St. Dominic's Church in Sheboygan, Wisconsin. Present at the wedding were my mother, all our brothers and sisters, their spouses, our entire combined immediate family of seven children and our friends from Milwaukee. It was a very small wedding. The only other people present were the best man, George Schmidbauer, his wife Lollie and my friend Vivian Tauschek, who was matron of honor. We went to Indianhead Mountain, in Michigan, for a ski honeymoon. Even though it was only November, it was extremely cold and nasty. On our way home we stopped in Oshkosh to see Richard who was in college at the time. From there we headed home to Sheboygan to begin our new life together.

We took the kids on family shopping trips to Milwaukee. I remember stopping at the Range Line Inn in Mequon on the way. The kids insisted that we stop because of their french onion soup. Harold started making it for the family because it became one of our favorites.

Harold was active in the United States Auto Club, where he was one of their officials. I always went along to watch the races. During one race I was on my way to the bathroom when I saw a big group of people gathered around a woman who was lying on the ground not breathing. I immediately started CPR.

The paramedics showed up, put her on a stretcher and took her to the medical tent. When she got to the medical tent, she was conscious and they thought she had heat stroke. I went back to my seat and continued watching the race. I was amazed when I saw the same woman walk into the stands and go back to her seat. I immediately went and talked to her husband and asked if he knew where she had been. He said she had been gone for a long time and he was worried about her. Once I told him I had just performed CPR on her, he immediately had an ambulance called. They put her in the ambulance and took her to the hospital. I do not know what happened after that. I hope she did well.

Chapter 17

Management Opportunities at St. Nicholas Hospital

In 1976 several major changes happened in my life. I married Harold and I was asked to take a management position at St. Nicholas Hospital. This required working full-time, which was now possible since the children were older and more self-sufficient. In management I learned even more intricacies of the medical profession. I had to try to please the doctors, administration, and especially the patients.

We were in the process of building a new hospital which was several miles from the current campus. This required many overtime hours for planning, prior to the move and for the move itself. After two years of planning and building, the move was set for January of 1979. Harold and I had planned a ski trip for February and I was assured by my boss, that this would work out just fine. At the last minute the date of the move was delayed and our ski trip was now in jeopardy. Since we paid for the trip up front, I was given the go-ahead for the trip. The night before we left, Harold and I were at the new hospital unpacking supplies including bed pans and urinals.

One of the things Harold and I enjoyed doing was downhill skiing. For many years we went to Vail, Colorado. A good friend of ours from Sheboygan, Paul Testwuide, was the head of the Ski Patrol at Vail. Because of this, we got to take part in some opportunities that most other skiers didn't get to partake in. The Ski Patrol closed a black diamond ski trail to the public so only our group could use this ski run. Harold was a beginner and they decided to take him down the black diamond hill. Our friends waited for him at the bottom. As they watched him come down, they laughed and said it was more fun than watching cartoons.

As we drove back to Sheboygan from our trip, we drove past the new hospital. We marveled at how great it looked all lit up and open for business. Within 15 minutes we were back at the new hospital. My daughter, Lynn, had had an accident and was in the hospital. This was not the way I expected to be introduced to the hospital in full action. Luckily, she recovered completely and even survived her mother's wrath after hearing about her foolishness which led to the accident with her car.

When Juli was in high school, she worked at the new St. Nicholas Hospital for a summer in the lab. One day I was taking a break in the cafeteria, which was below the lab, when the ceiling started leaking. We had to go around and put pails out to catch the water that was leaking down. We found out later, that one of the lab assistants forgot to put a hose into the sink, when cleaning the pipettes. I found out who the culprit was when I got home.

While I was working at St. Nicholas, my brother Bob came home from the service. He was my hero, and I did not want to leave his side. He was there for me personally and professionally. The song "Dear Richard" was popular at the time. Bob called me Richard as a nickname. While I outgrew this nickname as I became an adult, it somehow it drew us closer. When Ronnie died, Bob took me under his wing and we were very close buddies. I got him interested in skiing and he took me along to Vail. We spent many hours together, giving me the opportunity to air my thoughts and sorrows. I also became closer to his son Jim, who is one of my very dear friends today. I know that I can depend on Jim for anything.

Jim's first date with his wife, Phyllis was quite memorable and hilarious. Harold, Jim, and I were going to dinner and it was suggested that we ask Phyllis to go along. Phyllis was a nurse that I had hired to work at St. Nicholas Hospital. One Saturday night, the four of us decided to go to Milwaukee for a nice dinner. When we got to Phyllis's apartment Harold went in to get Phyllis. When she came to the door, Harold introduced himself as her date for the night. All Phyllis could think of was that I had set her up with an older gray-haired guy. She was not happy. To this day we still tease her about her first gray-haired date in Sheboygan. After that night Jim and Phyllis started dating and eventually got married. They have two sons and are grandparents.

Chapter 18

Nurse Supervisor Experiences

One of the interesting aspects of being a nurse manager is working as the house supervisor on weekends and holidays. We had an administrative person on call if we ran into any difficult situations and needed assistance. We all took our turn and had many interesting experiences along the way. I received one call from a woman who was having a party and didn't have enough silverware. She wanted to know if she could borrow some from our cafeteria. Another woman called to see if we could provide her with helium to blow up balloons for her child's birthday party.

The week before moving to the new hospital, I was the supervisor at the old hospital while the other hospital managers served as hosts for an open house at the new building. I answered a call that came into the Obstetrics Department. A young woman was in labor and she and her fiancé wanted to get married in the hospital chapel before the baby was born. Their reasoning was, the baby legally could be given the father's last name if they were married. Since this was an extremely unusual situation, I called the new hospital to discuss the idea with the administrative person on call. When I called, I found out there had been a fire in the hospital. Thankfully the fire was minor and didn't cause any damage.

I decided to let the couple go ahead with the wedding. I never heard of any repercussions regarding the situation. To my knowledge this was the only wedding ever held in the original St. Nicholas Hospital Chapel.

It was never dull working in a management role. One morning we got a woman in as a patient. She had a punctured internal ileostomy pouch. To do a pouch internally was a new and experimental procedure. The closest hospitals that were knowledgeable regarding this procedure were in Marshfield, Wisconsin, and at the Mayo Clinic in Rochester, Minnesota. Her physician preferred that she be transferred to the Mayo Clinic. I spent the late morning and early afternoon planning for an air ambulance transport from the Sheboygan airport to the Minneapolis/St. Paul airport. From there she would need to be transported by ambulance to Rochester. As the arrangements were being finalized, Minnesota was hit with severe thunderstorms and flooding. The road from the Minneapolis airport was under water and an ambulance would not be able to get through. We could get her to Minnesota, but they were unable to get her to the hospital in Rochester once she was there. We had scheduled a plane to pick her up at 5:30 that afternoon. Our only option was for her to take a helicopter from the Minneapolis airport to the Mayo Clinic. This was on a Thursday, which was the day of my golf league. At approximately 5:50, while I was standing in the middle of the fairway, I saw a Lear Jet leaving the Sheboygan airport heading north. I knew that my entire day of preparation had worked out and she was on her way to a place that could give her the medical care that she needed.

Now that I was in a management position, I began to think about the fact that I only had a diploma in nursing. One of the job requirements was a bachelor's degree. Since I had never gone to a regular college it was time to look into advancing my education. At about this same time Judy McClutchy, one of my nursing school friends from Milwaukee, told me about some classes that were being held in Milwaukee. St. Francis College of Joliet, Illinois specifically designed the classes for diploma graduates who wanted to earn a degree. I drove to Milwaukee along with two friends to attend our first class. We had some horrendous trips due to snowstorms and bad weather, but we were determined. I was very grateful to my mother who always watched the kids for me while I went to class.

During the semester I contacted the college and asked what it would take to get them to provide classes in the Sheboygan area. They told me they would need a place to hold the classes and a commitment from at least 30 students. They would publicize the classes and hire professors from Marquette University, Lakeland College, the University of Wisconsin, Sheboygan, and the Green Bay campus.

I approached the administration at the hospital, where I worked. I asked for the use of a classroom in which to hold the classes. I provided the argument that improving the education of their employees would benefit the hospital overall. The college advertised the classes in the local and area newspapers. Approximately 35 students applied immediately. I found out later, because I had done this, I was considered the local contact for the college. I got my tuition for half price for all the classes I took that were held in Sheboygan. Cutting my driving time from an hour each way, to five minutes each way certainly was a major benefit for me and all the other students. I received my Bachelor of Arts Degree from the College of St. Francis in May of 1978.

I had always felt insecure in my management position because I didn't have my degree. There was always the possibility that the administrative representative would change. If that happened the new boss could insist on the managers meeting all the job requirements. I now met the criteria.

After several years, I decided it was time again to pursue higher education. I considered an MBA from the University of Wisconsin-Milwaukee. I also heard of a program being offered by the University of Wisconsin-Oshkosh. The program was being designed for experienced working individuals. The degree was a Master's in Public Administration with three facets to choose from: Law Enforcement, Community, or Health Care Administration. I chose Public Administration.

Much of the work was self-study. There were additional classes through teleconference at the Sheboygan campus. There were also videotapes of classes, with papers to be written regarding the information presented. Sometimes sessions were held on campus on Saturdays which allowed students to continue with their work schedules.

One class I took was on Health Care Economics. This was my most difficult class because I took it as an interim class. It was held on campus for both bachelor and graduate students. The difference was that the graduate students had to write a lengthy paper as one of the class requirements. The class was in January, for three weeks, from 8:00 a.m. to noon, Monday through Friday. Since I was working full time, it meant driving to Oshkosh early in the morning and getting back to work at 2:00. I worked until 10:00 p.m. and repeated the process the next day.

Because I had a supportive boss who believed in what I was doing, I was able to adjust my workday for the class. The biggest obstacle I was facing was finding the time to write the paper while working full-time, taking classes, and raising my children.

A classmate and I approached our professor and asked if we could teach one of the last classes and present the actual hospital budget. Our plan was to present the three parts of a budget: Capital, Supply, and Full-Time Equivalents for employees. After defining these, we would show how the budget was followed for the year and how expenditures were justified. The professor accepted our request and allowed us to do the class in lieu of writing the paper. Because the budget was something we did on a day-to-day basis, it took no time at all to make a few transparencies for our presentation.

After we completed the class, numerous students came up and said they learned more on that day than they had during the entire three-week period. We were sure the actual practical application was a lot more interesting and helpful than just following the examples. As a result, I got an A+ in the class.

In October of 1983, on a Thursday afternoon, I was called to the Administrator's office. My immediate response was that I had done something wrong and was being fired. Why was I filled with guilt and didn't give myself the benefit of the doubt? My initial response to something out of the ordinary was negative instead of positive.

The Administrator explained that the nun who was the Administrative Assistant had a heart attack and it was not known when she would be back. The hospital accreditation survey was due within a few months and the nun was also working on several other projects. He wanted me to work in her position to keep these projects viable until she was able to return to work. I had until the next morning to decide. I went home in shock and discussed it with my husband, Harold. We decided it was a great career move for me. On the following morning I found myself sitting in a big office in administration with a secretary at my disposal. I had no idea what I was doing or what I was supposed to do. It didn't take long before I was fully involved in my responsibilities.

One of my first jobs while I was in this new position was to organize "St. Francis Day". This was an educational program that all employees were required to participate in. The first presentation was for the administrative team and it was presented by members of the corporate office. It was a two-day session on what is important in life, self-worth, and the importance of each individual and their individuality. Twenty to thirty employees attended at once and the program ran for about nine months to get as many of them to attend as possible. The program was extremely well accepted by the employees. I observed many of them in tears as they watched some of the videos and listened to the presentations. We even had requests to attend a second time, but with so many employees, this was impossible.

By the middle of January 1984, it was determined that the nun who I was filling in for would not be able to return to her position. I was promoted to the permanent position of Administrative Assistant. I was glad that I was in the graduate school program because I was again in a position with a job description that required a master's degree. Somehow throughout my career, I was put into positions and then rushed to get the educational requirements needed to keep that position.

Another educational presentation I had to put together for the administrative staff, and all the managers, was in leadership skills. The sessions were a week-long. During one of the sessions I was put in charge of a task force to solve the problem of transporting patients around the hospital in a timely manner. Our group worked diligently on this for the week. At the end of the week we were told that since this was a major problem, we were to continue our work until we came up with a viable solution to the problem. Since I had to do a thesis to meet my requirements for graduation, I petitioned my advisor to allow me to use the project as a basis for my leadership class thesis requirement.

The major determination we made as a task force was that before we could find a solution, we had to better define the problem. We hired a temporary person to do a major time study of all movement and transportation of patients and supplies, including administration and discharge. This provided valuable information as to exactly where the problems were. The result was that we hired a transport coordinator who managed all the volunteers to do the major movement of patients throughout the hospital. Prior to the implementation of the program, 62 percent of patients were transported by nursing staff. With the use of transporters this number was decreased to 3 percent transported by nursing staff. From then on, only when the condition of a patient was severe was a nurse needed to be in attendance while they were being moved.

This program is still being utilized to this day. The nursing staff can be more efficient and attentive to patients with medical needs.

The time spent in solving this major dilemma was clearly justified. Money was saved and patients were taken to their appointments and returned to their rooms in a timelier manner.

The following year the American Association for Hospital Planning sent out a memo requesting entries for new projects within health care facilities. I requested permission to present our transportation system. Although I did not receive the evaluator's vote for the Planning Award, my project was considered "sufficiently creative and innovative". I received a Letter of Recognition from the American Association for Hospital Planning. By special vote, I was awarded a check for $500. This was to let me know that among those who submitted applications, which were found deserving of a Letter of Recognition, my project represented the most innovative achievement.

On January 18, 1985, I received my Master's in Public Administration from the University of Wisconsin, Oshkosh. I again had the official education for the position in which I was employed. This had been a long and tedious course of study. It was a joint effort because while I was taking classes, Harold did all the cooking and laundry, among other household chores and activities. I came home from work and went into the living room and studied or wrote papers until dinner was ready. After eating I retired to the living room to work until bedtime.

I didn't work on the weekends, that was time for the family. My course work and assignments were tedious tasks, but I am pleased I stuck with it. This accomplishment provided the proper credentials for future endeavors.

I went to a meeting at our sister hospital, St. Vincent's in Green Bay with Karen, a woman I worked with. On the way back Karen was driving and we hit some bad weather on highway I43. It began hailing and raining hard. Suddenly we saw a flash on the hood of the car and all the lights on the dash flashed on and then went out. We coasted to the side of the road just as a semi went zooming passed. It stopped in front of us. The driver jumped out and came running back to our car. He looked at us through the front windshield. Karen opened her door and started to get out. He gasped because he thought for sure we were dead. He saw the lightning strike the middle of the hood of the car and bounce up to the top of the car. He called a tow truck and they came and hauled the car in. I have no recollection of how we got home. All I do remember is that the next day I had trouble getting out of bed. It was like I had no strength in any of my muscles.

When I got to work I looked for Karen. She told me she had the same sensation so we must have taken a good zapping of lightning. The weak sensation lasted for several days and then just went away.

In about 1980, several years after Harold and I were married, we got an invitation to visit Cooper Communities in Arkansas. They were developing a new community. Harold's daughter Tammie and my son David came along on the trip. As we drove from Little Rock to Hot Springs Village we thought we had made a major mistake. The houses on the side of the road were very rundown. We joked about going back to Little Rock for a hotel if the accommodations weren't acceptable.

Once we drove into the village we were impressed with the beauty and the aesthetics we saw. We stayed in a 3-bedroom home and greatly enjoyed our visit. We literally fell in love with Hot Springs Village on that trip and knew that this was where we wanted to retire. We purchased a lot that same weekend.

In 1992, we took a golf vacation with friends Grace and Ken Wirth to Hot Springs Village. While we were there, we had dinner with friends, Ruth and Harry Knight, who were previously from Sheboygan and had moved to the village. Harry asked Harold when we were going to move to the village. Harold told him, "Find Dorothy a job, and we'll move."

The next day Harry brought over the newspaper and told Harold he should find a job for me. While looking at the paper, Harold called to me, "There's a perfect job for you here. You have all the job qualifications, and it's in Benton." Benton was only about 25 miles away.

The next morning I called Saline Memorial Hospital in Benton, who had posted the ad. The position they were looking to fill was for the Assistant Administrator. They told me they were planning on making an offer to someone else that day but would like to talk to me. I told them I was on a golf outing and had no clothes to wear to a job interview for an executive position. They told me they understood and I should come in anyway in my golf clothes. Of course, I did.

My interview lasted for several hours. The next morning we left for Sheboygan. The following week I had to go to Minneapolis for a meeting. I planned on spending the weekend with Juli and Richard, who were both living there at the time.

On Thursday I got a call from Harold while I was at the hotel in Minneapolis. Harold told me the people who interviewed me wanted to talk to me immediately in Arkansas. I called and they informed me that they wanted me to be in Arkansas on Saturday to interview with the Board of Directors and the Board of the Medical Staff.

I told them it would be almost impossible to make the arrangements. They said they didn't care what it would cost, I should make the arrangements. I flew back to Arkansas Friday night, interviewed all day Saturday and flew back to Minneapolis Saturday night.

Richard picked me up at the airport. We went out to dinner

and laughed about the whole situation. When I got back home to Sheboygan, Harold and I talked. What if they made an offer? Did we really want to move to Arkansas this soon? We decided if it was a good offer, we were going to make the move.

On Tuesday I got a call asking me what I wanted for a salary. Once we agreed on that they asked me what else I wanted. I asked for four weeks of vacation. Lynn was getting married that spring and my mother was elderly and I knew I would have to make trips back and forth because of her. I also asked for immediate health insurance coverage. They agreed to all my requests.

At that same time, I was scheduled to have carpal tunnel surgery. After my surgery I handed my resignation in to the administrator of St. Nicholas Hospital in Sheboygan. I informed them that I had accepted a job in Arkansas.

During that time, David was traveling with friends in Europe. I informed him that we were moving from Sheboygan to Arkansas. He wrote me a letter telling me that he was upset about no longer having a home in Sheboygan. With the letter he also sent me this beautiful poem.

Dorothy Meletta George

My Mother

From Adam's rib she became
And I from her arrived the same.
She gave me a home and a place to grow
The importance of that I'll never let go.
She taught me to be sensitive
She taught me to be tough
She told me that life would sometimes be rough.
But never give in is the example she gave
A lesson that I will forever save.
She's there when I'm happy and when I'm sad
She was there for me when I missed my Dad.
She was the water and the sunshine
That made the seed grow
And in her, all my love I bestow.
For me there could never be any other

The she in this poem, is you, my mother.

Chapter 19

Our Move to Arkansas

In December 1992 I was hired by Saline Memorial Hospital in Benton, Arkansas as the Assistant Administrator reporting directly to the CEO. They paid for our moving expenses and the storage of all our furniture for 10 months while we built our house. It was a sweetheart deal that we couldn't turn down. We had planned on moving to Arkansas in a couple of years for our retirement anyway. Saline Memorial Hospital was a private hospital owned by Quorum Corporation. When deciding on my start date we agreed to wait until after the Christmas holidays so my first day of work was January 5, 1993.

While looking for a place to live, I asked the CEO of the hospital if he wanted us to live in Benton where the hospital was located. I told him I would prefer building our retirement home in Hot Springs Village where we owned property. He was very enthusiastic about this. He wanted to establish a health care presence in Hot Springs Village and the surrounding areas for hospital coverage. Saline Memorial was the closest hospital.

I worked long hours five days a week. Harold spent his

time looking for lots. He found a lot on the 15th hole of the Balboa Golf Course. We had already started working with Cooper Community on house plans. As soon as the sale on the lot was final we began building. The man who oversaw the building project was from Wisconsin and all he talked about was Leinenkugel beer. Every Friday Harold brought the crew a 6-pack of Leinenkugel beer. This kept them very happy, since Leinenkugel was not readily available in Arkansas. The construction went very well. We moved into the house in October 1993. I was at a conference in Hot Springs during the move-in date so Harold had to oversee the move on his own. The first night we could sleep in our new home, Harold was alone because I was out of town in a hotel.

After we moved to Arkansas, we greatly missed not having a dog. We dog sat for a Bichon-Friese many times for some good friends. We found we loved the breed because it was loving and intelligent. I started looking for a new puppy and we found a litter in Little Rock, Arkansas. We contacted the owners and proceeded to negotiate. I ended up buying a little female puppy. Harold didn't know anything about this, so I didn't bring the puppy home right away. The next Saturday was Valentine's Day. A friend of mine, Joanie Wallace and I drove to Little Rock in the morning to pick up the puppy. Later that day I heard Harold drive into the garage from work. I put the puppy in a big box in the guest bedroom. I put a red ribbon on her head. When Harold came into the house, I told him that his Valentine's Day present was in the guest bedroom. I told him it was very expensive, and I could not return it so he better like it. He went in the bedroom, looked at the puppy in the box, and just stood and stared at her while she looked back at him. I finally said, "Pick her up, she's real." He picked her up and cuddled her for the longest time. She weighed less than two pounds at that point. We named her Molly and she became an important part of our family. When Harold "took her for walks" he rode in the golf cart and she ran alongside attached to her leash. She got a good walk, but Harold didn't. After several years our sweet cuddly puppy started becoming vicious. She attacked me one night and we decided we could not keep her. We took her to the vet who diagnosed her with Alzheimer's. At 12 years of age, she was put to sleep.

We had a big deck off the back of our house. We made planters out of big round floral plant containers and used these for growing herbs and vegetables. The herbs were used in all our cooking. When they were ready to harvest, we tied the stems together and hung them up to dry in the house. We stripped the leaves off the stems, put them in Ziplock bags and stored them in the freezer. This supplied us with herbs all winter long.

One summer morning I was thrilled to see a perfectly big ripe, beautiful tomato growing in one of the pots on the deck. That afternoon I was sitting in the family room reading a book when I saw a squirrel run across the deck. He carried that tomato in his mouth and ran to a tree that was next to the deck. The squirrel jumped to the tree and up he went to one of the high branches. It was at least 20 feet high. There he sat happily eating my ripened tomato. I called my friend Nell and asked her when squirrels started growing tomatoes in oak trees in Arkansas. We had a good laugh about this.

When Gayle Coy and I first met and started a friendship, we took hikes at Petit Jean State Park. We talked a lot about our kids and joked about how fun it would be if one of them got married in the park. As time went on this became more of a possibility than we had expected. Her son, Steve and Juli started dating. They met when they were both visiting in Arkansas and hiked at Petit Jean State Park. Years later, when they got engaged they decided to have the wedding on September 29, 2001, at Petit Jean State Park.

When Harold and I were together partying one night with our friends we all discussed how fun it would be to pitch in and help with the wedding. After discussions with Juli and Steve, it was decided that the gals would do the cooking with Lynn supervising and the guys would do the serving and bartending. Juli and Steve hired a minister from Little Rock to perform the ceremony. They made arrangements to rent all the necessary items for the wedding dinner which would take place in the pavilion. The only people present were immediate family, friends of Juli and Steve, and our friends who helped prep, bartend, and serve the dinner. The ceremony, day, and evening were beautiful. Everyone had rented cabins at the park so we could all be together for the weekend.

After about two years, the CEO who had hired me took a different job in another state. A new CEO was hired. After a period of time, I had nurse managers in tears in my office. They told me they felt they were being sexually harassed by the new CEO. I reported him to the Quorum HR manager and an investigation was made. It was determined that even though some of the things that he said and did may have been inappropriate, it was not sexual harassment.

One year and one day after I reported the CEO's behavior, his secretary called me to set up a meeting that afternoon at 4:30

in my office. I knew what was coming. I was fired immediately and was walked out the door. They never really gave me a clear reason why I was let go. Given the timing of when they fired me, I highly suspect that it was due to the harassment that I had reported. A member of the Board of Directors, came with me as I cleaned out my desk and walked me to my car. They told me I could come back the next day to pick up any personal items I had in my office. That was the last day I was ever in Saline Memorial. I worked for them for approximately 3.5 years.

Chapter 20

QUALvue

Saline Memorial Hospital is owned by Quorum Corporation, a for profit corporation that owns hospitals. Shortly after I was fired from Saline Memorial, I was approached by them to do consulting work. They were looking to hire me to prepare hospitals for JCAHO (Joint Commission Accreditation Hospital Organization) and work as an interim Director of Nursing (DON) while they were hiring someone for the opening. I did several long-term positions covering when someone was either fired or became ill.

While I was doing consulting, I developed a process for making the JCHCA (Joint Commission on Health Care Accreditation) an easier process for hospitals to attain their accreditation. I started my own business called QUALvue Consulting. I traveled around the country setting up policy and procedure manuals for hospitals according to the Joint Commission Standards. I did this until I retired in approximately 2001.

Throughout my nursing and consulting career I was always bothered by the fact that hospitals worked diligently for months before a JCAHO evaluation to have everything in perfect running order. As soon as the survey was completed, they fell back into their old processes after they received their accreditation score. This type of regression had no benefit for the patients or residents. This was the core reason I started QUALvue Consulting. Keeping everything in perfect running order was the right thing to do beyond just passing the survey.

As the owner of QUALvue, I provided hospitals the assurance that they would receive an A+ accreditation from Joint Commission after their survey was completed. To accommodate this, I went to the hospital for three days. I went through all the policy and procedure manuals, and made sure things were getting done according to the written process. I made a list of recommendations that needed to be corrected. I returned to the hospital two to three months later to make sure they had corrected the policies and procedures that had not been performed up to standard. Once the changes were made they were ready for the Joint Commission survey.

One night we had an emergency while I was filling an interim Director of Nursing position in Emporia, Virginia. I got a phone call around 5:30 a.m. that there had been a major accident on Interstate 95. A bus on a Freedom Trail Journey filled with high school students had crashed. The Freedom Trail Journey was a way of re-enacting the journey slaves took to flee the South. Each year local schools sponsored these field trips to educate their students. Apparently, the driver fell asleep, went off the highway, down an embankment, and into the river. One young man was trapped under the bus and drowned. He was one of the counselors on the trip. Rosa Parks was called and flown in to identify him. We later found out he was Rosa's godson. She was very close to him since she never had children of her own. I spent several hours with her trying to console her, listening to stories of her godson.

We spent the day in the gym and cafeteria of the high school. There were plates of food on the table. I remember her looking around, taking a donut, wrapping it in a napkin, and putting it in her purse. She seemed like a typical little old lady. She would have been in her mid 80's at the time. This was in Oct. 2005.

The students that were on the bus lost everything due to the fast-flowing river. Some of the nursing staff was assigned to go to the department store to pick up clothing for the students. Rosa helped us sort the clothing and hand them out.

While covering an interim Director of Nursing position in Whiteville, North Carolina I ran into an unusual situation. Since we were on the East Coast, we had some severe storms, including hurricanes. Late one afternoon there were severe hurricane warnings. The CEO called me into his office to tell me he was headed home because his wife was afraid of storms. He told me I was in charge and to do whatever was necessary to take care of the situation. Being from Wisconsin originally, I had no experience with hurricanes. I immediately started to gather information from the local staff. I determined preparations were not much different than what we did for a snowstorm in Wisconsin. I notified all the patient care areas and support staff departments that we needed two shifts in each area to cover for the storm. I was told we may need coverage for 5-7 days. Having two shifts staffed meant one set could sleep while the other was working. The kitchen staff informed me that they had made sandwiches ahead of time and they were leaving to get home prior to the storm hitting. I immediately informed them they would need two shifts staffed as well.

One of the pharmacists wanted to go home because his wife was 8.5 months pregnant. I told him to bring her to the hospital. I thought she'd be safer there than at home. She was assigned a room and the staff had fun with the situation. They even put mints on her pillow at bedtime.

When I looked out the window that evening the wind was so strong the rain was coming down horizontal. The only real problem we had with the storm was the water coming in the windows and doors. The laundry staff got bedspreads and blankets and laid them across the bottom of the windows to soak up the water. They brought huge laundry containers and brought the wet ones back to the dryers. They continued through the night to keep the place dry. As it turned out, we got through the storm perfectly without any problems. We ended up not needing the two shifts, but I'm still glad we had them both there in case it turned out worse.

Several days later, on a Saturday, I flew back to Wisconsin for a Packer game on Sunday. As we drove down the streets of Wrightsboro, North Carolina to go to the airport I was amazed at the number of trees that were cut off about 10 feet high. When I got to the airport they were still functioning on auxiliary power. My plane was the first one to leave the area after the storm.

I was called to fill an interim position at a Quorum hospital in

Emporia, Virginia. They were in the process of hiring a new Director of Nursing. An external applicant asked if I would have lunch with her. She felt that since I was not an official hospital employee, I would be more upfront about the position they were seeking to fill. We went to lunch and started the usual small talk. I asked her where she was from and she said Laurel, Mississippi. I was astonished. I asked her if she knew my former CEO. The one who fired me. She said she did not know him personally but knew of him. She told me he kept his motorhome parked in the employee parking lot at the local hospital. Then what she said shocked me! She told me you could often see young nurses joining him in it over lunch. I could not believe that this was the same CEO that was cleared of sexual harassment of nurse managers in Arkansas.

Another weather-related experience during my time with QUORUM happened in Oklahoma. There were severe tornado warnings in the area when I landed. I picked up my rental car in Oklahoma City and drove to the western part of the state. As I drove down the highway there were no other cars in sight. Looking ahead, the sky was cut in half, black to the south and white to the north. The radio warned of severe thunderstorm and tornado warnings for certain counties but I had no idea what county I was in. Since no other cars were on the highway, I must admit I was speeding a bit. I think I was on I-40 and thought that if I sped fast enough, I would drive out the storm.

I got to Sayre, Oklahoma safely and checked into my hotel. Knowing I was settling in for the night, I ordered room service for dinner. After I had eaten, I decided to put my tray out in the hall. As I was setting it down a gust of wind blew the door shut behind me. I was out in the hall in my pajamas with no key to get back in. I had to go down to the front desk to retrieve a new key, much to my embarrassment.

The next day I heard all the harrowing stories about the tornado. One woman's husband was working as emergency staff after the tornado. He told her he found a man who was driven headfirst into the ground, with just his legs sticking up. Unfortunately, there were numerous deaths in the area. Several days later when I flew out of Oklahoma City, you could see the devastation the path of the tornado took around the city.

Chapter 21

Things I've Made

Over the years I have never been able to sit idle. I always had a project I was working on. When the kids were little I made most of their clothes. I also made many of their toys and accessories. Here are some of the projects I took on.

1. **Barbie Dolls**
I knit many matching outfits for the Barbie dolls. I sewed little outfits for them including, but not limited to, dresses and pajamas. I think the most unique were the two-piece bikinis I knit for them.

2. **Christmas Stockings**
The summer Richard was born, I was out shopping and saw a kit for a knit Christmas stocking. Since he was born in July, I decided I could have it made for him by Christmas. At that very moment, a Christmas tradition began. From then on, each one of the children had a homemade Christmas stocking made for them with their name knit into it. After Ronnie, myself, and all the children had their stockings, I continued knitting stockings for extended family, nieces, nephews, and their families. I also

made some for friends and their children. I told Aunt Sue that if I had known she was going to have 13 children, I would never have started with her family! Of course, I am proud that her son, my nephew, who is a former Wisconsin alderman, has a knit Christmas stocking with his name on it that I made for him. I must have made at least 75 of them.

3. Sewing

Having three girls in our family in junior high and senior high school kept me busy. It was difficult when they all went to different proms. I made each one a new dress for each of their proms. They never wore the same dress twice or wore the same dress their sister wore.

We enjoyed skiing as a family and I made several down ski outfits. They included jackets, bibs, and gloves. I made a down jacket and down sleeping bag for Richard. We were all well dressed in all the appropriate clothing.

4. Afghans

Another tradition for the kids was for me to knit an afghan for them when they went to college. This turned into a bigger project than I had planned. I knit one for my grandson, Bryan. He came home one weekend and asked me if I would knit him another afghan. He told me every time he wanted to use his afghan, he had to wrestle it away from his roommate. As a result, I ended up knitting one for his roommate and one for a friend of my grandson Steven's.

5. Sloppy Joes

St. Dominic School did not have a hot lunch program for its students. If someone wanted to eat lunch at school they had to bring their own. I didn't have time to volunteer for school activities, so I volunteered to do a hot lunch program as a treat for all the children. I shopped on Wednesdays and got everything prepared. Thursdays I served hot lunch to all the students. This occurred once a month. The menu was sloppy joes, chips, and Jell-O. The mothers from different classrooms were assigned to bring cupcakes. The children loved it! One young boy always came up to me after lunch and thanked me for the delicious lunch.

6. **Knitting**

One time when I didn't have any particular project to work on, I saw a pattern for a full length, multi-colored dress. It was beautiful. I decide to make one. It was not something I would ever wear so I gave it to a friend of mine. She was very happy to receive it. In addition to this project I knit numerous sweaters over the years.

Chapter 22

Different Paths for the Family

Through the next years, the kids all attended college. Richard attended UW-Sheboygan Center, UW-Stevens Point, received a Bachelor's degree from UW-Oshkosh and got a Master's degree from UW-Madison. Lori attended UW-Sheboygan Center and UW-Whitewater where she got her Bachelor's Degree. Lynn attended UW-La Crosse, left school, and moved to Minneapolis. Juli attended UW-Sheboygan Center, UW-La Crosse and got her Bachelor's Degree from the University of Minnesota.

Richard lived in the Minneapolis area at the same time that Juli and Lynn were there. While working, Lynn met a friend who was originally from California. She talked Lynn into moving back to California with her. David struggled his first year of college at UW-Sheboygan Center. He decided to move with Lynn to California. He worked for several years and then attended the University of California-San Diego where he got his Bachelor's degree.

The Kids

Over the years the kids got married.

Richard married Sarah Turcotte. They have a son, Joseph Casper Manser, born in 2004. He is named after his great grandfather and great-great grandfather. Richard is a hydrogeologist and is a leader in his field.

Lori married Gary Lacy. They have three children: Bryan born in 1986, Steven born in 1989, and Jenna born in 1992. After being a stay-at-home mom, Lori pursued her career as an IT Manager.

Lynn moved back to Sheboygan from California in the mid 1980s. She was between jobs, planned to be in Sheboygan for a short time, but met her future husband, John Shovan. After they got married in 1992 and worked very hard to open Lake Street Café, a restaurant in Elkhart Lake. They eventually divorced but continued to run the restaurant together. John passed away October 24, 2021. Lynn still lives in Elkhart Lake. They have two children: Jake born in 1996 and Sydney born in 1998.

Juli married Steve Coy. They have two children: Sabin born in 1999 and Galen born in 2000. Steve passed away May 23, 2012. Currently Juli is a Director of Photography living in western Wisconsin, working out of the Twin Cities.

David married Stephanie Noonan in California. David and Stephanie live on Balboa Island in Southern California. They have three children: Hannah born in 2009, Molly born in 2010 and their "little surprise" Lilah, born in 2012.

I have two stepdaughters raised by their mother. Harold George's children are Terrie born in 1966 and Tammie born in 1969.

Terrie married Dan Cobian in Sheboygan, WI, right after graduation from high school. They divorced shortly thereafter. Terrie married Mike Meyer, and they are also divorced. Terrie has two children: Eric Cobian born in 1984 and Kelsie Meyer born in 1994.

Terrie has been at Rockline Industries for 19 years and has a title of Rockline Maryland Logistics Asset Leader. She lives in Sheboygan Falls with her puppy, Comet. She teaches Turners, a program for children to learn acrobatics. She also teaches volleyball and has been doing that since high school. Terrie's son Eric was in the Marines for a time and was sent to Iraq three times. He has received the NAM (Navy and Marine Corps Achievement Medal) three times. He also serves for the Marine Corps Color Guard. He works for DND Carpeting. Her daughter Kelsie spent five months in Ecuador teaching Spanish while she was in high school. She received her Bachelor's and Master's degrees from the University of Minnesota. She is teaching Spanish at public high school in Andover, Minnesota. She also coaches girls' volleyball. Her significant other, Ryan, also received his Bachelor's and Master's degrees from the University of Minnesota. He teaches History in a high school in Minneapolis.

Tammie has worked several jobs over the years and is presently working at Rockline Industries also. She is currently living in Sheboygan.

Chapter 23

Packer Fans

Harold and I went to almost every home Packer game. While living in Hot Springs Village, we made the road trip to Green Bay whenever possible. We met many great people thanks to attending these games. Barb, Dennis, Mona, and Larry were the two couples with season tickets who sat in the row ahead of us.

After the games we'd head to a bar in De Pere for a drink or two while we waited for the traffic to clear. There was an elderly patron who was there every week. He played the piano and the whole bar sang along.

As Green Bay Packer Season Tickets Holders we were put in a lottery with the chance of purchasing two tickets if the Packers ever made it to the Super Bowl. In 1998, the Broncos played the Packers in San Diego in the Super Bowl. Harold and I got the opportunity to purchase tickets, which we did. We attended the game. While in San Diego, we stayed with David and John Reichert, my nephew. The Super Bowl experience was unbelievable. Even though the Packers lost to the Broncos 31-24, nothing you see on TV compares to being there in person.

Chapter 24

Memorable Trips I've Taken

Hawaii

Harold and I went on a cruise in Hawaii. It was pretty low key. We did some short trips such as whale watching and we saw some shows, like teaching people how to dance the hula. In the evenings there were performers who entertained us on the boat. In the morning someone drove them back to where they had boarded the boat the evening before. The weather and scenery were spectacular.

Germany

In December of 1984, Harold and I took a trip to Germany. We started in Munich and arrived in time to attend the very popular Christmas Markets. We then got on a boat and went down the Rhine River for several days. We got on and off the boat throughout the trip. We hiked through the Alps one day and at night we danced, sang, had dinner, and then we got back on the boat. We traveled while we were asleep to the next location. When we woke up, a day guide took us through different areas. We spent time in Oberhausen. They brought in entertainers for cocktail hour and after dinner.

One of the Christmas Markets was held in a small chapel. This chapel was where Silent Night was written. According to the story told to us, the priest wanted a new song for midnight mass on Christmas that year. Two of the priests sat down and proceeded to write Silent Night and it never lost its popularity.

We also went to Oberammergau. When I was about 11 years old, I had a pen pal, Ursula Lauble, from that town. We were the same age. Apparently, we were relatives and my Aunt Anna arranged for us to write to each other. I communicated with her for several years and she sent several packages to me. One of the packages contained a couple of small gold dishes. I sent her a lot of shoes, clothes, and food because it was during the war and they didn't have a lot of these things. I think that is why she sent me knick-knacks as gifts. To this day I enjoy taking out her letters and reading them. Unfortunately, we were not able to see her when we went to Oberammergau.

Greece

In May 1995 I travelled with my sisters, Gert and Catherine, to Greece to meet up with Juli and Steve who were vacationing there. The five of us went on our own and took buses and trains to see the countryside. We got there on Juli's birthday. That night we sat across from the Acropolis in a park and enjoyed wine while we celebrated. We also took ferries to several of the islands. It was a wonderful trip. (Appendix G)

California

In 2001, while I was consulting, I had a job at a hospital just outside of Phoenix. Harold and I flew there and then when I finished the job, we rented a car and drove to Las Vegas. We spent a couple of days there and then headed to California.

We drove along the coast, stopping at Pebble Beach, toured The Hearst Castle, and made several other stops along the way. We stayed at a place that was on a peninsula jutting out into the ocean. It was beautiful. We ended up at David's, who was living in San Diego. He was living with John Reichert at the time. John had a sailboat. We went sailing on the ocean and watched a sailboat race. We eventually drove back to Phoenix and visited some of Harold's racing friends before we flew back home.

Many years later, in 2015, I took a trip to California for my 80th birthday. All the kids brought their kids and we rented a house in Palm Springs. We had a fabulous time celebrating and we really got to spend quality time together.

Chapter 25

Health Issues

In 2004 I started experiencing weakness in my legs and other medical problems. I saw numerous physicians in Arkansas, and no one could figure out what was going on. I went to the Mayo Clinic in April of 2005. After enduring seven full days of miscellaneous tests, they told me there was definitely something wrong, but they didn't know what it was. They told me to go home and try physical therapy and if it didn't get better to come back again and they would pursue more testing.

After several months, my symptoms went away and my family practitioner told me she thought I had a virus of some kind. I had been tested for Lyme's disease and West Nile disease and everything came back negative. My physician said there were numerous viruses out there that were still active.

In October 2012, my legs were getting weaker, which led me to see another physician. He ordered a biopsy of my knee and had me walk up and down the hallway. Just by my walking and seeing the trembling in my hands he knew what was wrong. I was diagnosed with Parkinson's disease.

Chapter 26

Social Activities in Hot Springs Village

I continued with my social activities and different volunteer commitments that came up. One thing I did was completely revamp the Hole-In-One Program for Hot Springs Village Women's Golf Association in Arkansas. I was lucky enough to have a hole-in-one on the 17th hole on Cortez Golf Course. It is one of the most beautiful holes in the village.

I love golf and board games like Mahjong and Rummikube. A typical day for me was to have a tee time in the morning, meeting the ladies at the course to play 18 holes, either with open golf or league. After the golf game we'd have a drink, visit at the bar, and discuss how our game went. Then we'd go to someone's house for heavy hors devours, a cocktail, followed by a game of Mahjong. We also tried to include other activities in our daily lives. A group of us went on a cruise and toured local small towns, but no matter what we did it always ended with a game of Mahjong.

Christmas has always been a special time of year for me. I've always looked forward to the preparations and decorations that made the entire house feel so festive. I've always tried very hard to find special gifts. I especially liked making personal gifts for everyone, so they could be displayed over the years. I believe in preserving the memories that the sight of the gifts bring back.

It was hard for us when we moved to Arkansas. We weren't always able to get home to Wisconsin for Christmas. We decided we had to start new traditions to fill the years that we and our friends were missing with family. One year we planned a dinner for Christmas Eve and invited all our friends who weren't going homes for the holidays. The next year we did it again, which started a new tradition of spending the holidays with our friends from the Village. Harold and I did the cooking and we chose the menu. For hors d'oeuvres we made black olive and onion cheese spread, with rye crisps and a Swiss cheese mixture melted on top. Harold was known for his wonderful Caesar Salad, which was followed by twice baked potatoes. (Appendix D) He prepared Steak Diane tableside. (Appendix E) For dessert we had flaming bananas foster.

The first year we had the dinner, we all sat at the table for several hours. We told jokes, stories, and enjoyed good wine. By the end of the night, we drank all the wine we had in the house. The following year we had each couple bring a bottle of red and a bottle of white wine for the dinner. During a typical year we had anywhere from 12-16 people sitting around the table.

Chapter 27

Moving Back to Wisconsin

In 2015 our children convinced Harold and I to move back to Wisconsin. We sold our townhouse in Arkansas and moved into an apartment in Sheboygan. The complex was designed for retired seniors so there were always a lot of things going on. A few years later we both made the move to Pine Haven Christian Home, Prairie Crossing-Assisted Living. Harold was diagnosed with prostate cancer and passed away October 26, 2016. I am now living at Pine Haven Christian Home in Sheboygan Falls, WI.

Chapter 28

Final Chapter

I am 86 years old and the member of a large, beautiful family. I have 5 beautiful children and 2 stepchildren that I wouldn't trade for anything. All of them have meant the world to me my entire life. They have supported me in everything that I have ever decided to try.

As you can see, we are one happy family that supports each other fully and enjoys being with each other. God has been very good to us. We've had our joys and sorrows over the years, but it has been a wonderful life with good relationships.

Dear Friends and Family,
I hope and pray that you have learned well how to love and respect others. May you have as happy and fulfilling a life as I was fortunate enough to have. I send love to all my friends and family. I want to thank God for all the blessings He has bestowed upon us. Always be there to love and support each other. There is nothing that will ever replace friends and family. My love to all of you.
Love, your friend Dorothy
Love, Mom

Appendix A

Ice Cream in a bag

1 C Half & Half into small Ziplock bag
1.5 teaspoons vanilla extract
1 T sugar

Seal bag firmly and get excess air out. In a larger Ziplock bag fill halfway with ice. Put smaller bag with cream into the larger bag with ice. Seal both bags firmly and get out excess air. Top off with extra ice. Shake bags around to mix up ingredients and put into freezer.

Appendix B

Homemade Root Beer

2 oz. McCormick's Natural and Artificial flavored Root Beer concentrate.
5 lbs. sugar
5 Gallons warm spring water, 95 degrees F
1 C pre-boiled water cooled to 85-95 degrees
1 package (1/4 oz/7grams) dry active yeast

1. Clean and sanitize all bottling equipment according to information below. Shake root beer concentrate well. Mix with sugar in a large container. DO NOT USE ALUMINUM! Stir in Spring Water.
2. Dissolve yeast in 1 Cup pre-boiled water. Allow yeast to dissolve undisturbed, 10-15 minutes. Add to sugar mixer and mix well.
3. Bottle immediately into plastic bottles leaving 2-inch space at top of bottle. Cap tightly. Store each bottle on its side in a warm place, 70-80 degrees F for 1-2 days. Then store upright in refrigerator at 40-45 degrees F for additional 3-4 days. Keep refrigerated and consume within 7-8 days. Makes 80 servings.

Appendix C

Sauerbraten

Combine 1 cup cider vinegar, 1 cup regular vinegar and 1 cup water. Pour over meat (venison or beef roasts). Be sure the meat is covered. Slice 3 medium onions over top. Add 1 1/2 tablespoon peppercorns, 10 to 12 whole cloves and 4 to 5 bay leaves. Marinate for 1 week turning meat daily.

When ready to prepare pour off juice and save. Brown meat in heavy skillet. Salt. Brown onions from the marinade in butter. Add some of the saved juice to onions and bring to a boil. Pour over the meat. Roast covered in 325 to 350 degree oven for 2 to 2 1/2 hours until tender. Cut into serving pieces and put meat into serving dish (keep hot in oven). Thicken juice with flour or cornstarch mixed with water. Add about 1 teaspoon sugar to gravy. Pour in 1 cup cream. Strain gravy. Pour gravy over meat. Serve very hot. (It helps to warm the plates in the oven).

Appendix D

Harold's Caesar Salad

3/4 cup olive oil
cloves of garlic
1 package croutons
1 head crisp torn Romaine Lettuce Juice of 1 fresh lemon
1/2 teaspoon salt
Freshly ground pepper
2 eggs coddled 1 minute
1/2 cup grated Parmesan Cheese

Pour oil into small bowl. Crush 2 garlic cloves and add to lemon juice and olive oil. Let stand 30 minutes to 1 hour. Add coddled eggs and stir well. Set aside. Fry minced garlic slightly in olive oil. Brown croutons slowly until browned in this garlic oil. Cut a clove of garlic in half and rub well into salad bowl. Toss lettuce with dressing, fresh ground pepper, Parmesan cheese and croutons ending with croutons on top.

Appendix E

Steak Diane

Tenderloin Steak cut into 3 to 4 ounce size pieces
Fresh black pepper
Soy sauce
Olive oil

Trim all fat and gristle from steaks. Pound steaks to enlarge them and to reduce them to a 1/4-inch thickness. Rub steaks with Soy sauce, olive oil and pepper. Roll up each steak and arrange on a platter. Garnish with parsley, cover and refrigerate until serving time.

For cooking at table:

A small pitcher olive oil and plate with 1 stick butter
Minced shallots or scallions and fresh parsley in small bowls
A pitcher containing 1 tablespoon cornstarch blended with 1 tablespoon Dijon mustard and 1 cup beef bouillon.
Worcestershire sauce
A lemon cut in half
Cognac, Port or Madeira

Pour 1 tablespoon oil into the frying pan. Add 2 tablespoons butter. Butter will foam up, gradually foam will subside and just as butter begins to brown, unroll one steak and immediately a second in the pan. Sauté 30 to 40 seconds on one side, turn with forks or wood paddles and sauté on the other side. Steaks will barely color and will just become lightly springy to the touch for rare. Rapidly roll them up with your forks and replace on the platter. Sauté the remaining steaks in the same manner.

Add another spoonful or two of butter and when foaming stir in a big spoonful of shallots or scallions and parsley. Let cook for a moment then stir in the pitcher of bouillon mixture. Stir for a minute then add a few drops of Worcestershire and the juice of half lemon (pierce lemon with fork, picking out seeds first and squeeze with flourish). Add droplets of cognac and Port or Madeira, taste and add droplets more again with flourish.

Unroll each steak and bathe in the sauce, turning and dipping with your two forks before placing on a hot dinner plate. Spoon with additional sauce.

Appendix F

Bananas Foster

3 tablespoons brown sugar
2 tablespoons butter
1 large ripe banana, peeled and sliced lengthwise
2 tablespoons banana liqueur
2 ounces white rum
1 tablespoon lemon juice
1/8 teaspoon cinnamon

Sauté banana in sugar and butter until tender. Sprinkle with lemon juice and dust with cinnamon. Add banana liqueur and rum and set aflame, basting the banana until the flame dies out. Wonderful spooned over vanilla ice cream. Serves two.

Appendix G

Greece Trip Travel Log

Friday - 05/26/1995:

We arrived in Athens at about 10:00 a.m. We were through customs by about 11:00. Juli and Steve were waiting for us when we got through customs. I was lucky to be there since I almost missed the connection in New York at JFK Airport. The plane was supposed to leave Atlanta at 1:15 but left at 3:00 because the flight crew was delayed in Florida. I got to JFK and the agent took all the Athens passengers directly to the gate. Gert and Catherine were getting a little nervous that I wouldn't make the flight.

When we got to the hotel, we found we didn't have a reservation at the Titania. We found a room at the Grand Hotel. It was just fine. We settled in our room and then took the subway to the Plaka, an old historical neighborhood in Athens. We walked from there to the Acropolis. Everything was already closed for the day, but we walked around the area and could still see a lot. We went shopping at George's jewelry shop (friend of Steve's). We also spent time shopping for jewelry, drinking beer and Ouzo. We had dinner at the Plaka and then headed back to the hotel for the night.

Saturday - 05/27/1995 - Juli's Birthday:

We went to the Acropolis most of the day. It is extremely impressive, especially the frumpy maidens! After the Acropolis we went back for a siesta. Then we headed back to the mountain across from the Acropolis and drank some wine as we watched the sunset. After dark we went down to a restaurant for dinner and watched the lights change over the Acropolis.

Sunday - 05/28/1995:

We had breakfast at the hotel, it consisted of bread and yogurt with honey. We went to Syntagma Square where we saw the parliament, changing of the guards, and Hadrian's Arch. We walked in the park and then went back for a siesta. We went to the 7:00 p.m. mass at the Cathedral. They were having First Communion. The children receiving First Communion were carrying lit candles and began using them like swords. I was afraid someone was going to get burned. There were candelabras in the back of the church. They were the big brass holders with holes for the candles. There was a big brass tray underneath to catch the wax. The people brought in several candles, even up to a handful, lit them, and put them into the candelabra. It was very crowded!

We were going to go back to the place where we had lunch to have dinner and listen to Greek music. The man was going to teach us how to do Greek dancing, but we settled on dinner and drinks at a corner café.

Monday - 05/29/1995:

We checked out of the hotel and took a bus to Corinth. The bus was filled with high school students on their way home from school. We talked to them as they were dropped off at villages. One boy kept trying to carry on a conversation with us. Was it a bet? Lots of laughing and "goodbyes". We felt that the others were challenging him to talk to us. They were practicing their English.

When we got to Corinth, Gert and I went to look for a room while the rest stayed with the baggage. We found a hotel. The man who signed us in asked where we were from. He had a former girlfriend from Appleton, Wisconsin.

We spent the rest of the day on the waterfront. In the evening we went back to the waterfront for drinks, dinner, and Greek dancers who were performing in the Square.

Tuesday - 05/30/1995:

We went to ancient Corinth and toured the ruins. Steve found a bone; we don't know what kind it is. There were people there who were digging in one area. He asked them but they didn't have a clue. They told him that they found many bones. Of course, there were many comments about Steve's bone. He has written all the places that we have been to on the trip on his bone.

We caught a train at 1500 to Pirgos and then took another train to Olympia. The train ride covered the entire coastline of the Peloponnese Peninsula. There was water on one side and mountains on the other. Beautiful flowers grew wild and in gardens everywhere. There were many orange and lemon trees. The countryside was very hilly with houses built on many levels and heights. They were all stucco with tile roofs and flowers mainly roses, grew in fenced in yards.

We arrived about 8:00 p.m. and stayed in a room near the train station. A lady met us at the station and offered the rooms for 6500 drachmas for all three of us, this comes out to $29 American which is really cheap. Juli and I looked at the rooms, but it turns out she only had one room. She sent us with a young girl to another place for the second room. The second room was bigger and better for the three of us. When we were negotiating for the second room, Juli was trying to communicate with the man at the tavern that the three of us would be staying in that room. It wasn't working. I got involved and pointed to me and said two "seesters". I pointed to Juli and then to the other place. He understood right away.

There is a taverna in the building next to the room that the three "seesters" shared. We sat for a couple of hours drinking beer, wine, etc. Juli and Steve never showed up so Catherine, Gert and I had soup and cheese pie and then walked into town. We toured the area, found a liquor store, and bought some Ouzo. We went back to the patio by our room and had Ouzo and water. Juli and Steve showed up. They had been there earlier looking for us. We all drank until it was late in the evening. The man staying in the other room got up and complained and asked us to be quiet. He said he had a long day and wanted to get some rest.

Gert and Catherine went to bed. Gert had done her laundry (underwear) and had hung it on the line by the patio. Juli and Steve moved the line down to the taverna and took pictures with the locals all laughing at Gert's underwear.

When I went to bed, Gert was still awake. We had a good laugh at Catherine's snoring. Then Gert went to sleep, and I had noise in harmony, toots, and snorts.

Wednesday - 05/31/1995:
We got up about 9:00 a.m. to shower but there was no hot

water. We walked into town for breakfast. We bought three different pastries and espresso. Great pastries! We shared so that we could all try the different things. Then we met up with Juli and Steve. We toured the Olympic Ruins, what wonderful history. We walked across the Olympic field. A group was having a makeshift race. They were enjoying running in the "Olympics".

We took a bus to Pirgos. At 3:40 we caught a train at Pirgos (Nypros) to Patrai (Natpas). There we caught a bus to Delphi. The scenery of the countryside was great. Roses grew everywhere plus little wild red, purple and yellow flowers. There were chickens and goats in the yards. We saw rows of flowers in yards separated by paths.

We changed our plans and in Patrai we caught a bus to Rios and then took the ferry across the bay to Andiron. From there we took a bus to Nafpaktos. We found the Nikh Hotel about six blocks from the bus stop. Gert and I went in search of the room while the rest stayed with the luggage. A little old lady was at the hotel. She had one gold tooth on each side of her mouth. She spoke no English at all. We negotiated the price for the room with Drachmas in hand. Later when we got to our room, we found rates on the back of the door for more than double what we negotiated. We will probably have to pay more in the morning. In the morning the manager just handed me my passport and thanked us. We didn't have to pay any extra.

We went down to the wharf, picked up a big bottle of wine, beer for Gert, and some gyros. We sat up on an old fort eating our supper. A beautiful star lit up the sky. It was late at night and yet there were kids all over the place. When we got back, Juli and I sat out on our balcony and talked.

Thursday - 6/01/1995:
We went to the wharf and picked up pastries, fruit, and coffee. We sat on the steps on the Square eating our breakfast, then caught a bus to Delphi. A man met us at the bus, offering rooms to let. He took us to the Athena Hotel. Our rooms overlooked a valley, a distant mountain range and body of water. It looked like the port where we came in. We could see villages in the far distance and on the waterfront. What a breathtaking view. It was too late in the day to go to the ruins. We took a cab to the monastery. This was an ancient monastery where four monks still live. Juli and Gert had to put on skirts and Steve had to put on long pants before they were allowed in. The gold mosaics over the walls and ceiling were beautiful.

Gert, Catherine, and I went out to dinner after which Gert and I went to a piano bar. Later Juli and Steve joined us.

Friday - 06/02/1995:
We had breakfast at the hotel and then went to the Delphi ruins. They are built into the side of a hill/mountain. It was awesome. I think they were the best so far that we have seen. We made it all the way to the top. It took several hours to do so. Halfway up we ran into a group of children with their teacher. They wanted to practice their English. We talked for a while. The teacher said she wished they would pay as much attention to her as they did to me.

About 3:30 we had lunch and rested a bit. At 5:30 Gert and

I went to the lower ruins. Catherine was too tired and her knees hurt. We ran into Steve and Juli there. They had hiked down into the valley. We picked up a couple of bottles of Retsina and beer to party on the deck overlooking the valley. We all went for dinner, then we went back and partied some more.

Saturday - 06/03/1995:

We picked up fruit and pastries and had breakfast on the balcony overlooking the valley. In the distance we could hear the chimes and bells of goats being herded way down in the valley.

We took a bus to Chalkis (Khalia). We couldn't get a connection to an area with ferries, so we took the train to Athens. Then we took a local bus to the bus station where we caught a bus to Rafina, on the coast. A lady told us where to make the connection. She told us we also could take a cab, but to bear in mind that we would get ripped off. We found a nice hotel overlooking the water with mountains in the background. It was beautiful with the cruise ships in the dock.

Gert and I went out at about 11:00 p.m. and had a Greek salad. We woke Steve and Juli up for a nightcap.

Sunday - 06/04/1995:

We caught an 8:00 a.m. ferry to Mikonos, arriving about 1:00 p.m. We were met (swarmed) at the dock by dozens of people trying to rent rooms (rooms to let). We got a place down the coast. The lady's name who rented us the room was Artemeulah, Diane in English. Once we were settled, we went to the town Centre where we picked up some fruit and wine. We also had a Gyro for lunch.

Gert, Catherine, and I went to the beach. It was quite a hike up and down hills from our place but by now we are used to it. When Gert and I got back from the beach, Juli, Steve, and Catherine were all sleeping. While sitting on the veranda looking out over the sea I could see the mountains from another island in the background. Everything was white stucco with blue, red, or green shutters. The flowers were unbelievable. The geraniums were at least 7 feet tall; they looked like a tree. The terrain was like a desert. The roads were lined with stone walls. The area was very hilly, and everything was built into the side of a hill facing the water. We went to Niko's for dinner. Gert had her calamari (squid). We tried the baked custard. The waiter brought us Metaxa from the owner. Steve waved him over and he came and had a nightcap with us.

Monday - 06/05/1995:
What a bad night, we were eaten by mosquitoes and kept awake by Catherine's snoring. Juli and Steve got up at dawn to watch the sunrise on a distant hill. They rented mopeds to explore the island. Gert, Catherine, and I went into town. We walked all over the Centre. We saw the famous windmills. We took the wrong bus back to our room but got to see Paradise Beach. It is known for alternative lifestyles, but Gert wouldn't walk to the beach holding my hand. We went down to our beach when we got back. Gert and Catherine swam while I slept. Gert got daring out in the water and took her top down so that she could say she went topless in Greece. She had Catherine as her witness.

Juli and Steve got back from Island exploring. We had "gimlets" and sat on the veranda watching and enjoying the view. We also had cheese, tzatziki, bread, and crackers. We went back to NiKo's for dinner. We like Niko's because he serves us Metaxa on the house after dinner. Another interesting feature is that all the lights are in the shape of a boob! Only in Greece!

Juli and Steve had a walk on the beach without us. I don't know why?!?! We went to bed because we had to get up early because of nervous Catherine. Juli lit a punk for mosquitoes. Steve was chasing them with a towel and whipping the walls.

Tuesday - 06/06/1995:

We caught a 9:00 a.m. ferry to Ios. We now carried Ouzo, red wine, and vodka on the ferry. We also had lots of bread, salami, tzatziki, tomatoes, and crackers. We stayed outside until 12:30 and then had to move in out of the sun. Juli and Steve took another picture of Gert with her "beer me" sign while she was sleeping.

We arrived in Ios at 2:15. We walked up to the church on the hillside for an overview of the island. We then caught a 3:30 ferry to Santorini. The large sailboat was anchored, and we passed it with the ferry. It was quite a sight to see. The view of Santorini as we approached was breathtaking. Santorini is composed of five separate volcanic islands in a circle. It is thought that the center was the original volcano which formed the present structure when it erupted. The towns are built on the top of the volcanic remains. In the distance you see a mountain of black, sheer cliff with the white stucco structures of the town at the very top. The drive up from the boat in a bus was unbelievable and the view was incredible. It is impossible to describe how high up we were on a pile of rocks where the villages are built. The capital city Fira, is the first village at the top. This is the capital of Thera, the island on which we are staying.

We took another bus to Fero Sephani where we found a place to stay. We decided to splurge a bit and found a villa overlooking the sea. The cost was 18000 drachmas which is about $27 per person. It had a lovely patio, stove, refrigerator, table, chairs etc. It also had a swimming pool. The beaches on Santorini are an hour bus ride away so the pool won us over. It was too much money for Juli and Steve, so they got a room up the hill. Gert, Catherine, and I decided we had worked hard enough and would pamper ourselves. One drawback was the double bed in the loft. Gert and I had to sleep together while Catherine had the single on the first floor. We gave in to age over youth and to her snoring. The only way to get to the place is down a long sloping stairway. What a trek just to get to our room. We thought that there had to be another way, such as a road, however there wasn't.

We could see the sailboat that we passed earlier with the ferry anchored in the sea below our villa. After watching a beautiful, breathtaking sunset (of which Gert took 73 pictures) we went out to dinner to a nice restaurant on the top of the hill. We treated Juli and Steve for dragging us around all over Greece. The waiter messed up the order and Steve never got his dinner. He brought us a dessert platter of fruits and ice creams and an extra bottle of wine as an apology.

Wednesday - 06/07/1995:

We all slept late and then spent the day walking around. We went to Fira, the capital of Santorini. There were lots of shops, markets, etc. The streets are all hills with stairways from one street to another. We got back to our room about 3:30 and spent the rest of the afternoon at the pool. Juli and Steve went hiking to the top of a hill overlooking the sea.

When they got back, we had cocktails and snacks poolside. Gert ran out of beer and had to go all the way up the hill to replenish her supply. She never walked that far and high for a beer! We watched the sunset again and then went to a little café for dinner. This time Steve got to eat also. After we got down the steps, Gert and I remembered that we had a bet from earlier in the day. I lost so I owed her a Metaxa. We did not want to walk back up, so I went to the reception area to see if they were serving drinks. They had a little bar inside. The lady told me they weren't serving but she would see if she could find something for us. She opened the refrigerator and said she was sorry but there was no wine there. I told her that we were looking for some Metaxa. She grabbed a half full bottle from the shelf and gave it to me. She told me we should enjoy it in our room. Gert, Catherine, and I sat on the patio having our nightcap, watching the stars.

Thursday - 06/08/1995:

Another beautiful day, only a bit cooler. We took a bus tour of the island today. Several cruise ships were anchored in the sea below our villa. Also, several sailboats were out because there was more wind today.

Some of the walls of stone that have been constructed were built into a straight cliff. Did they have cliffhangers build these? The walls of the island are sheer drops to the sea.

We walked into Fira for the bus tour. The first stop was the monastery at the top of the mountain, the highest spot on the island of Santorini. Next, we went to the ruins of Akatiri which was a village destroyed in 1700+ BC by a volcanic eruption. It was found in 1967 by a Greek archaeologist. Some of the buildings were very well preserved. The original buildings were covered with volcanic ash, not lava, which is why they were so well preserved. No human remains were found. Also, all the gold, silver, jewelry, and anything of value had been removed. Therefore, the theory is that the village was evacuated prior to the eruption. 8000 ceramic pots have been found so far. The roads are smooth and well laid. The beds have been replicated from casts of the originals. You can see the drainage plumbing under the streets. There was a bathroom in the main room with a slab for a toilet with a hole and pipes that lead down to the drainage system. The frescoes that they found were moved to the museum in Athens. "The Boys Boxing" and "The Fisherman" were the major ones. Next, we went to Perissa Beach. This is a black beach made up of volcanic ash. We had lunch there. Gert went swimming in her bra and underpants. "No fool like an old fool." After lunch we went to the winery. We enjoyed the good wine. The wine museum was excellent with very interesting old wood and iron wine crushers. There was a lot of ancient equipment.

We went back to the pool while Steve and Gert went up the hill and got us gyros for dinner. We played Uno for a while.

Friday - 06/09/1995:

We had to get up early to catch the ferry to get back to Athens. Steve did the bull work and carried the bags up the hill. The "seesters" were on their own. What a trek! We took a taxi to the port. The ride down the hill in the cab wasn't nearly as bad as going up on the bus. We caught the ferry leaving at 7:30 and spent the entire day on the boat. We stopped at Ios, Paros, and Siros. Nervous Catherine thought Paros was where we got off and came running when they announced the name.

There is a slight haze over the islands. Siros has a little different architecture and more color. The waterfront is lovely. The closer we got to Piraeus the more speed boats and sailboats we saw. We arrived in Piraeus at 6:15 and took the train to Omonia Square, back to the Grand Hotel. After getting settled we took the train to the Plaka. We shopped for a bit and then went to dinner at a restaurant at the foot of the Acropolis. The lights on the ruins were beautiful. Back to the hotel to pack and to bed.

Saturday - 06/10/1995:

Up at 5:15 since we had an 8:00 flight and had to be at the airport by 6:00-6:30. There were a lot of questions for the security check at the airport. It was tough to leave Juli and Steve. They were headed to Crete this evening. Steve wants to visit friends and they will be staying on a naval base.

We arrived in Frankfurt at 10:40. Catherine's flight to Los Angeles was in an hour but Gert and I had until 1:30 before we left for Cincinnati. The Frankfurt airport was beautiful! It is new and many areas were still under construction.

The prices are atrocious. Gert paid eight dollars for 2 cups of coffee.

We all got home safe and sound.

Overall thoughts regarding Greece:

The exchange rate was approximately 223 drachmas to one dollar.

Plumbing - the showers are small square fixtures with about a 3-inch edge around and a handheld nozzle. Many times there was no hot water. It felt like washing a whale in a thimble but after two weeks we mastered it without flooding the bathroom.

The water closets (WC - toilet) - no paper was to be disposed of in the toilets. Also, it was smart to carry paper because there were times when none was available.

Culture - the people are very primitive in farming. You see donkeys with double baskets caring produce, etc. to market, especially in the islands. In Greece the kids ran around in the evening and watched the boats in the harbor. In Wisconsin they play street games, such as Kick the Can.

In Delphi we saw a truck full of fish on the street. The man was selling the fish right out of the back of the truck, a scale was hanging on the side.

Elderly ladies all in black are the widows. No one else wears black.

There was no tipping, but a cover charge was always charged which includes bread and water.

During the entire time we never ate inside, we always ate at outside cafés. We were never bothered by bugs or flies while eating.

About the Author

Dorothy Meletta George started developing her interest in writing later in life. Whenever she tells others about her experiences, she is encouraged to put her stories in writing. She has lived most of her life in Wisconsin but spent 20 years in Arkansas. She also spent short periods of time working in several other states. She returned to Wisconsin with intentions of being closer to family.

www.ingramcontent.com/pod-product-compliance
Lightning Source LLC
Chambersburg PA
CBHW040847240426
43673CB00020B/428/J